# THOREAU THE PLATONIST

# American University Studies

Series V
Philosophy
Vol. 10

PETER LANG
New York · Berne · Frankfurt am Main

Daniel A. Dombrowski

# THOREAU THE PLATONIST

PETER LANG
New York · Berne · Frankfurt am Main

**Library of Congress Cataloging-in-Publication Data**

Dombrowski, Daniel A.
  Thoreau the Platonist.

    (American university studies. Series V, Philosophy ; vol. 10)
    Bibliography: p.
    Includes index.
    1. Thoreau, Henry David, 1817–1862—Philosophy.
  2. Plato—Influence. 3. Philosophy in literature. 4. Philosophy,
  American—19th century. I. Title. II. Series: American
  university studies. Series V, Philosophy ; v. 10.
  PS3057.P4D66     1986          818'.309          86-10621
  ISBN 0-8204-0364-4


CIP-Kurztitelaufnahme der Deutschen Bibliothek

**Dombrowski, Daniel A.:**
Thoreau the Platonist / Daniel A. Dombrowski. — New York ;
Berne ; Frankfurt am Main : Lang, 1986.
    (American university studies : Ser. 5, Philosophy ; Vol. 10)
    ISBN 0-8204-0364-4

NE: American university studies / 05

Printed by Weihert-Druck GmbH, Darmstadt (West-Germany)

# TABLE OF CONTENTS

INTRODUCTION                                                    1

CHAPTER ONE:        THOREAU'S PLATONIC SOURCES                  5

CHAPTER TWO:        THE PLATONIC STRUCTURE OF

                    THOREAU'S UNIVERSE                          23

CHAPTER THREE:      THOREAU'S DIPOLAR THEISM                    75

CHAPTER FOUR:       THOREAU, SAINTHOOD, AND

                    VEGETARIANISM                               111

CHAPTER FIVE:       THOREAU AND THE PLATONIC

                    FUNCTIONS OF LANGUAGE                       167

BIBLIOGRAPHY                                                    203

INDEX                                                           215

# INTRODUCTION

William Wordsworth said to Ralph Waldo Emerson in 1848 that if Plato's Republic were published as a new book it would unfortunately have few readers, yet "we have embodied it all."[1] "We" refers at least to Wordsworth himself and Emerson, but probably also to Samuel Taylor Coleridge, the Cambridge Platonists, and Thomas Taylor, all of whom Henry David Thoreau read and admired. Wordsworth's Platonism is well known, but alas!, not Thoreau's. Wordsworth refers to "Plato's genius," his "lure sublime," and the "everlasting praise" due to him. Plato's truth, in Wordsworth's words, is that "half of truth" most neglected in England.[2] Yet it may come as a surprise to some that Thoreau is no less complimentary of Plato and no less chagrined that a Platonic spirit is largely absent in America.

I will argue for Thoreau's Platonism in five steps. In Chapter One I will treat the sources available to Thoreau that led him to become a Platonist, and in Chapter Two I will outline the conceptual structure to Thoreau's universe, which I allege is Platonic. Chapters Three and Four will detail features of

Thoreau's thought in what I think are highly original ways, with Plato once again receiving his just due. The former chapter is an analysis of Thoreau's theism, the latter of his vegetarianism. The final chapter provides insight into the Platonic functions of language for Thoreau.

When possible I will use the new Princeton editions of Thoreau's works (referred to by the title of the book in question, for example, Walden); otherwise, I will use the reprint of the 1906 edition of Thoreau (referred to as Writings).

## NOTES: INTRODUCTION

[1]See David Newsome, _Two Classes of Men: Platonism and English Romantic Thought_ (London: John Murray, 1974), p. 9.

[2]Ibid., pp. 26-27.  Also see Melvin Rader, _Wordsworth: A Philosophical Approach_ (Oxford: Clarendon Press, 1967), pp. 72-73.  The other half of truth was the Aristotelian tradition of empiricism.

# CHAPTER ONE:  THOREAU'S PLATONIC SOURCES

Kenneth Cameron[1] and Ethel Seybold[2] have done important work detailing Thoreau's familiarity with the Greek and Roman classics, and Seybold in particular has emphasized the extent to which Thoreau's "quest" was largely that of a classicist trying to recapture the glories of Greece.  Yet neither Cameron[3] nor Seybold notices much of Plato's influence on Thoreau.  Seybold goes so far as to claim:  "Reading philosophy, he had found no answer to his questions.  Plato... had given him dogma, not a way of life."[4]  On the surface, this claim is odd in that Plato's dialogue style does not easily lend itself to dogmatism, especially since it is Plato's own theories (in the mouth of Socrates) that are often criticized in these dialogues.[5]  But even on Seybold's own theory this claim is implausible, as is her belief that "Thoreau...was not interested in any metaphysical solution of the universe,"[6] since many of the features of Thoreau's mind that she emphasizes do not originate from Homer, and only imperfectly correspond to Oriental thought or Christianity.  These features are, however, paradigmatic examples of what has

come to be called "Platonism" or "neoplatonism" in
Western culture. Consider the following passages from
Seybold in her description of Thoreau:

> Insight and sympathy would show him
> "the unseen in the visible, the
> ideal in the actual," the real in
> the eternal creation behind the
> apparent and temporary.[7]
> He was searching, of course, for
> that true and ideal world of which
> this is but a reflection.[8]
> He was, as he had always been,
> certain of the existence of "the
> other world."[9]

Anyone even remotely familiar with Plato's
dialogues will see these beliefs as Platonic
commonplaces. It is not unlikely that Thoreau received
these views by reading Plato or neoplatonists. Again,
paradoxically, Seybold points the way. Thoreau read
Porphyry and Iamblichus, neoplatonists who were
"required reading" for the transcendentalists.[10] And he
read Thomas Taylor's translations of Plato and the
neoplatonists, translations which were "favorites" of
the transcendentalists.[11] In addition, Thoreau wrote an

essay at Harvard titled "Fate Among the Ancients," in which he relied on Plato.[12]

Although I agree with Seybold in her position: "In Thoreau's mind the Grecian age was the nearest possible earthly approximation of this ideal world,"[13] I find it unfortunate that she did not see very much of Plato, the expositor of the ideal world, in Thoreau's writings. It is not surprising that other scholars, who do not completely share Seybold's enthusiasm for Thoreau's classicism, hardly mention Plato at all in their treatments of Thoreau.[14] One must also contend with the remarks of William Ellery Channing, who claimed that Plato read too slow for Thoreau, that metaphysics was Thoreau's aversion, and: "I never knew him say a good word for Plato."[15] One is tempted to give a flippant reply to Channing to the effect that all one has to do is read Thoreau carefully to see him often saying good words about Plato. These good words will be detailed in Chapter Two. That is, I am not claiming along with Raymond Adams that Thoreau is a centripetal thinker who appears to move away from his dearest concerns.[16] Thoreau himself takes us directly to Plato and Platonic concerns through citation of, or obvious allusion to, Plato. Even Channing admits that if Thoreau were born in the palmy days of Greece, under the auspices of Plato, this half-divine man would have founded his own school and given his own wise sayings in that he loved (Platonic) purity and sanctity.[17]

Regarding the possible objection that Thoreau read too little in Plato or about Plato to be a Platonist, there is a simple, if lengthy, reply that can be made if Cameron is used to document Thoreau's sources, in addition to those listed above[18]: Thoreau read book reviews on books about the ancients, including Plato; he took notes on a book full of Platonic speculation by Lydia Maria Child, Philothea: A Romance, a book which also dealt with Pythagoras; his notes on a 1634 mask, Comus, include reference to Plato; he outlined Joseph Marie de Gerando's Histoire Comparee des Systemes de Philosophie,[19] which included treatments of the presocratics, Socrates, Plato, Plotinus, Porphyry, and Iamblichus; he copied from Plutarch's Morals,[20] quotations to the effect that Plato is scarcely perceived until scholars become men, and that philosophy is a "spring of motion" which gives one an "inflexible resolution" rather than the lifeless imagery of statuary; he copied extracts from Heinrich Ritter's The History of Ancient Philosophy[21]; he may have read Andre

Dacier's The Life of Pythagoras,[22] which also deals with
Socrates; he must have read Marshall Tufts' works A Tour
Through College and The Ancient and Popular
Pneumatology,[23] which indicate that Plato was often
mentioned in Thoreau's Harvard curriculum, as well as
Pythagoras, Porphyry, and Iamblichus; he copied extracts
on Plotinus from Sir Walter Raleigh's Works; he copied
extracts on Plato from Ralph Cudworth's The True
Intellectual System of the Universe,[24] including
quotations dealing with Plato's Timaeus and Porphyry.
With all these sources it is no wonder that Thoreau
refers or alludes to Plato or neoplatonists so often.
And how odd that Seybold's list of quotations from, and
allusions to, Plato is so truncated![25]

My thesis in this book is that Thoreau's universe
has a Platonic structure. But I do not exaggerate the
importance of this claim in that, as Seybold rightly
notices,[26] Thoreau is a master of "Protean disguise,"
now appearing as a hermit, then as naturalist,
Orientalist, primitivist, rebel, and so on. Great
authors have a way of eluding our grasp when we try to
translate them into some other language. I am only
claiming that one way to look at Thoreau is to see him
as a Platonist, and that this long neglected approach

should take its rightful place alongside the more
familiar views that are common in other studies. (I will
give an extended treatment of how to interpret Thoreau,
especially in the wake of deconstructionist theories of
literature, in Chapter Five.) If Seybold is right[27]
that Thoreau did not care in the least where he got his
ideas, or what suggested them, then my thesis would
appear to be that Thoreau was a Platonist in spite of
himself. What is more likely, however, is that Charles
Anderson is correct when he states that Thoreau's
allusive style:

> ...can be deceptively simple, in the
> American tradition (inaugurated by
> Franklin) of the natural as opposed
> to the bookish writer. But the
> experienced reader learns to see
> through this homespun disguise to
> the body of learning buried beneath.[28]

In this book I try to encourage this experienced reader
to experience, perhaps for the first time, the numerous
passages where Thoreau refers to Plato or Socrates or
the neoplatonists, or to notions that obviously come
from these thinkers.

I will not offer an imperialist approach to Thoreau, but a minority view in an already crowded field.[29] Minorities, it should be remembered, <u>do</u> have rights of self-expression. I find it premature to claim that the transcendentalists merely "read" the classics without having "studied" them.[30] Norman Foerster, who makes this claim, nonetheless resorts, like Channing, to favorable comparisons between Thoreau and Plato to develop his thesis regarding Thoreau's intellectual heritage. Foerster is instructive, however, regarding how we ought to approach Thoreau:

> To determine with some precision
> what Thoreau derived from the
> movement (transcendentalism), to
> ascertain what in general his
> spiritual and intellectual heritage
> was, we have only to go to his
> writings, and there to seek answer
> to the questions: Who were the
> great minds, or the lesser minds,
> that he knew well enough to discuss?
> And what was it that he owed to
> those to whom he was largely
> indebted?[31]

Yet scholars have not noticed how often Thoreau cites
Plato, nor have they noticed how often he alludes to
Plato, and hardly ever have they noticed when Thoreau
writes in a Platonic vein.  The classics had "the
highest significance" for Thoreau's intellectual and
spiritual life, but Foerster means by the classics works
by Homer and the other poets, not Plato.

Foerster comes closest to giving an argument as to
why we ought to ignore the connection between Thoreau
and Plato.  He relies on a passage from Walden:

> I aspire to be acquainted with wiser
> men than this our Concord soil has
> produced, whose names are hardly
> known here.  Or shall I hear the
> name of Plato and never read his
> book?  As if Plato were my townsman
> and I never saw him,--my next
> neighbor and I never heard him speak
> or attended to the wisdom of his
> words.  But how actually is it?  His
> Dialogues, which contain what was
> immortal in him, lie on the next
> shelf, and yet I never read them.
> We are underbred and low-lived and

illiterate; and in this respect I
confess I do not make any very broad
distinction between the illiterateness of my townsman who cannot
read at all, and the illiterateness
of him who has learned to read only
what is for children and feeble
intellects. We should be as good as
the worthies of antiquity, but
partly by first knowing how good
they were. We are a race of tit-
men, and soar but little higher in
our intellectual flights than the
columns of the daily paper.[32]

What is noteworthy here is not that Thoreau "never"
reads Plato, as Foerster suggests. (I assume "never"
refers to Thoreau's stay at Walden Pond. Why would he
even take Plato's dialogues to Walden Pond if they were
not among his favorites? Because they were on his
"reading list"?)[33] The point that Thoreau makes here only
has sense against a background of his familiarity with
Plato. Thoreau assumes here that Plato is wiser, better
bred, and more exalted than we are; he assumes the very
knowledge of how good Plato is that he writes about.

From the evidence cited in this chapter, and from
that to be adduced in subsequent chapters, we can see
that there is no difficulty in fulfilling one's
scholarly duties with respect to Thoreau's Platonic
sources, which are of two sorts:  direct sources, as in
his reading of Plato and the neoplatonists in school or
after his school-boy years--these direct sources are
evidenced in his explicit citation of Plato and the neoplatonists; and indirect sources, as in the diffused
echoes of Platonic thoughts which were "in the air" in
the transcendentalist movement--these indirect sources
are evidenced in Thoreau's allusions to Plato and the
neoplationists.  The likelihood that these sources
greatly affected Thoreau will increase as their quantity
is noticed; thus I will avoid the post hoc ergo propter
hoc fallacy (that is, after this therefore because of
this).  But the study of intellectual origins is only
relevant to criticism if it illuminates meaning and
deepens feeling; it is precisely such illumination that
I will try to offer in the rest of this book.[34]  It is
not the fact of Thoreau's slavish imitation of Plato
that I am interested in, but the opposite:  the original
ways in which Thoreau adopts and uses Platonic themes.
Emerson's words are instructive:

If we encountered a man of rare
intellect, we should ask him what
books he read. We expect a great
man to be a good reader; or in pro-
portion to the spontaneous power
should be the assimilating
power....Our debt to tradition
through reading and conversation is
so massive....All minds quote. Old
and new make the warp and woof of
every moment. There is no thread
that is not a twist of these two
strands.[35]

In short, the real difference between the original and
the imitative writer is simply that the former is more
profoundly imitative,[36] as I will argue in Chapter Five.

NOTES: CHAPTER ONE

[1] Kenneth Walter Cameron, _Young Thoreau and the Classics: A Review_ (Hartford: Transcendental Books, 1975).

[2] Ethel Seybold, _The Quest and the Classics_ (New Haven: Yale University Press, 1951).

[3] It should be noted, however, that in this book Cameron is primarily gathering Thoreau's sources in the classics when he was at Concord Academy. Here Thoreau would have come into contact with Plato or Socrates in at least two books: _Selectae e Veteri Testamento Historiae_, Nova Editio (Londoni: Veneunt A. Millar, W. Law, et R. Cater, 1797)--see Cameron, _Young Thoreau_, p. 25; and Frederick Jacobs, _The Greek Reader_ (Boston: Hilliard, Gray, Little, and Wilkins, 1827)--see Cameron, _Young Thoreau_, pp. 26, 28, 33. Also, at Concord Academy Thoreau read much from Platonists like Cicero--see Cameron, _Young Thoreau_, pp. 8, 10, 11, 13, 15.

[4] Seybold, p. 39.

[5] See, for example, the _Parmenides_.

[6] Seybold, p. 41.

[7] Ibid., p. 8.

[8] Ibid., p. 9.

[9] Ibid., p. 61.

[10]Ibid., p. 16.

[11]Ibid., p. 41.

[12]Ibid., p. 25. Also see Reginald Cook, "Ancient Rites at Walden," in Richard Ruland, ed., Twentieth Century Interpretations of Walden (Englewood Cliffs, New Jersey: Prentice-Hall, 1968).

[13]Seybold, p. 73.

[14]See, for example, Walter Harding, The New Thoreau Handbook (New York: New York University Press, 1980), p. 96. Another author who does notice Thoreau's classicism, but not his Platonism, is Clarence Gohdes, "Henry Thoreau, Bachelor of Arts," Classical Journal XXIII (February, 1928).

[15]William Ellery Channing, Thoreau: The Poet-Naturalist (New York: Biblo and Tannen, 1966), originally published in 1902. See pp. 50, 58. On Channing, see also Joseph Millichap, "Plato's Allegory of the Cave and the Vision of Walden," English Language Notes 7 (June, 1970), p. 277.

[16]See Raymond Adams, "Thoreau and Immortality," Studies in Philology 26 (1929), p. 58.

[17]Channing, p. 307.

[18]Kenneth Walter Cameron, Transcendental Apprenticeship: Notes on Young Henry Thoreau's Reading

(Hartford: Transcendental Books, 1976), pp. 30, 46, 71, 107, 108, 126, 142, 163-170, 181-186, 218, 220, 277, 289, 294, 299, 378.

[19]Joseph Marie de Gerando, Histoire Comparee des Systemes de Philosophie, 2nd edition (Paris: 1822-1823), volumes 1-2.

[20]Plutarch's Morals, the translation by "several hands," 5th edition (London: 1718), 5 volumes.

[21]Heinrich Ritter, The History of Ancient Philosophy, translated by A.J.W. Morrison (Oxford: 1838-1846).

[22]Andre Dacier, The Life of Pythagoras (London: 1707).

[23]Marshall Tufts, A Tour Through College (1832) and The Ancient and Popular Pneumatology. See Cameron, Transcendental Apprenticeship, pp. 268-299.

[24]Ralph Cudworth, The True Intellectual System of the Universe (London: 1820), 4 volumes.

[25]Seybold, p. 137. Even the fine new editions of Thoreau published by Princeton do not index all of the places in which Thoreau explicitly mentions Plato; it is therefore no surprise that his allusions to Plato are mostly ignored. For one example among others, see Journal, volume 2, p. 6.

[26]Seybold, p. 1.

[27]Ibid., p. 20.

[28]Charles R. Anderson, The Magic Circle of Walden (New York: Holt, Rinehart, and Winston, 1968), p. 153.

[29]See William J. Wolf, Thoreau: Mystic, Prophet, Ecologist (Philadelphia: Pilgrim Press, 1974).

[30]Norman Foerster, "The Intellectual Heritage of Thoreau," in Richard Ruland, ed., Twentieth Century Interpretations of Walden (Englewood Cliffs, New Jersey: Prentice-Hall, 1968), p. 35. Originally published in The Texas Review (1916-1917).

[31]Ibid., p. 37.

[32]Walden, ed. by J. Lyndon Shanley (Princeton: Princeton University Press, 1971), p. 107. For yet more evidence of the availability of Plato to Thoreau see Walter Harding, Thoreau's Library (Charlottesville: University of Virginia Press, 1957), and Emerson's Library (Charlottesville: University of Virginia Press, 1967). Also look at entries for Porphyry and other related figures. Millichap, p. 277, rightly notices that it is hard to imagine Thoreau adverse to the poetic texture of Plato's dialogues, and hard to imagine that as a student of Emerson he was unfamiliar with Plato.

[33]Before Thoreau went to Walden Pond he stated in

his journal that if he ever got a chance to live in the woods he would read (great) books again. See Journal, volume 2, ed. by Robert Sattelmeyer (Princeton: Princeton University Press, 1984), p. 90.

[34] See Richard Altick, The Art of Literary Research (New York: Norton, 1963), pp. 79-91. Finally, Thoreau was familiar with Plato's attitudes on art through Sir Philip Sidney's The Defense of Poesy, as Cameron documents.

[35] Quoted in Thomas McFarland, Originality & Imagination (Baltimore: Johns Hopkins University Press, 1985), p. 15.

[36] I am paraphrasing a remark from Northrup Frye, ibid., p. 87.

# CHAPTER TWO: THE PLATONIC STRUCTURE OF THOREAU'S UNIVERSE

The passage from Plato which takes us to the heart of Thoreau's view of the universe is Republic (501B), the famous "two glances" passage. Here Plato makes it clear that human beings are sandwiched in between two worlds: (1) the eternal, divine world of immutably perfect Forms or Ideas, which are the non-material, non-subjective objects that we think about when we truly know (that is, have episteme), but which have an existence independent of our thinking of them; and (2) the temporal world of material flux, which is imperfect and can be "known" only through mere opinion (doxa). The job for a human being is to glance frequently in both directions: at Justice, Beauty, and the like as they truly are in the formal nature of things, and alternately at that which they are trying to reproduce in mankind and in the material world, which is the region of images and likenesses of God. My procedure will be to first examine Thoreau's treatment of the eternal, then the temporal, trying all the while to decipher the details of Thoreau's view of human nature, a view which, like a crying child, begs for both the eternal and temporal.[1]

That Thoreau believed in an eternal world, an other
world, is indisputable:

> Surely, we are provided with senses
> as well fitted to penetrate the
> spaces of the real, the substantial,
> the eternal, as these outward are to
> penetrate the material universe.[2]

That this eternal world is Platonic is indicated when
Thoreau tells us that it is more real than the material
world, a Platonic commonplace, and that one of our
astronomers for this "starry system" of substantial
entities is Socrates, Plato's great teacher.[3] The
bifurcation of these two worlds is not absolute,
however. The temporal world is a moving image of the
eternal one, but we only notice this in those indolent
moments in life when time stands still, as it were.
Thoreau sarcastically points to the ladies of the land
weaving toilet cushions "as if you could kill time
without injuring eternity."[4] The image of eternity
which moves is the present. The present is constantly
being thrown into that vast stretch of future moments,
while at the same time it is losing itself to the past:

> In any weather, at any hour of the
> day or night, I have been anxious to
> improve the nick of time, and notch
> it on my stiok too; to stand on the
> meeting of two eternities, the past
> and the future, which is precisely
> the present moment; to toe that
> line.[5]

For Thoreau there is a link between time and eternity
and that link is to be found in the human person. But
this link at times appears clouded in mystery, a mystery
which I will try to elucidate later:

> So far from solving the problem of
> life, Time only serves to propose
> and keep it in. Time waits but for
> its solution to become eternity.
> Its lapse is measured by the suc-
> cessive failures to answer the
> incessant question, and the
> generations of men are the
> unskillful passengers devoured.[6]

There is something divine about Plato's (or the
neoplatonic) ideal world that fascinated Thoreau:
"Lumen est umbra Dei, Deus est Lumen Luminis." This

Latin quotation from Sir Walter Raleigh is cited
favorably by Thoreau in two different places yet, as far
as I know, it has never received scholarly analysis.[7]
This is unfortunate for two reasons. First, even in
translation ("Light is the shadow of God's brightness,
who is the light of light") the meaning of the quotation
is not intuitively obvious. And second, an
understanding of the quotation takes us to the heart of
Thoreau's hierarchy of the universe in a way that might
not otherwise be possible. Thoreau makes no secret of
the fact that his quotation is an allusion to Plato's
myth of the sun,[8] which rests on a four-term analogy:

sun : physical vision :: The Good :

intellectual or spiritual vision

Without the sun we could not see natural objects, yet at
its apex the sun itself is too bright to be studied.
And without The Good (agathon) we could not truly know,
yet The Good itself cannot be adequately described, only
hinted at through symbols. The Good is the highest
object for Plato. It is perfectly good because it is
indivisible and immune to the world of becoming and
passing away. One can thus see why many interpreters of
Plato have identified The Good With God.[9] The Good is
needed for knowledge in order to guarantee that our

fundamental assumptions, from which all other knowledge
proceeds, are true. Without such a guarantee, even the
most secure claims to knowledge would only be hypo-
thetical.[10] What makes The Good difficult, if not
impossible, to describe is the statement in the Republic
(509B) that "the good itself is not essence but still
transcends essence in dignity and surpassing power."

In order to understand why The Good transcends
essence (hyperousia), the neoplatonist Plotinus must be
invoked, because whereas Plato only briefly talks about
The Good,[11] Plotinus builds an entire philosophy upon
it. Plotinus holds[12] that all multiplicity presupposes
a prior unity. As we proceed from multiplicity to
greater and greater unity, we are bound to infer the
existence of a complete unity. This is called The One
(to hen) by Plotinus, and later called God by those he
influenced. Plotinus is instructive in his stringency
regarding what we can say about The One, which is
derived from The Good of Plato. Strictly speaking, we
cannot say anything about it. To say that it is good is
to put it in a category with other good things (apples,
sex, cars, moral decisions), thereby making it a one
among many, and no longer The One. In fact, since it
would then be in relation to all of these other things,

it would become a multiplicity itself. Likewise if we
called The One powerful, beautiful, et al. We cannot
even legitimately say that The One exists, for to do so
would put The One on a par with all other objects that
can have existence predicated of them. Because we
cannot even say that The One exists, we must remain
silent if we wish to do justice to "it." Those familiar
with Thoreau's thoughts on sound and silence will notice
his similarity to Plotinus here. Those who do speak
about God, for Plotinus, should admit that they do so
inadequately, albeit necessarily.

Now we are in a position to appreciate the
quotation under consideration. For neoplatonists, God
can be spoken of and known only in the shadowy realm of
divine emanation. God's creative power is evident in
lesser degrees of unity throughout the cosmos. In
descending order, the three levels of divine emanation
for Plotinus are: (1) intelligence (nous); (2) life
(psyche)--including subhuman psyche; and (3) infinitely
divisible matter (hyle). The divinity (unity) we see in
these levels reminds us of the first part of the
quotation: Lumen est umbra Dei (Light is the shadow of
God's brightness). But what God is in itself remains
unknown, or beyond knowing, and ineffable not only

because God's effulgence is the "light of light" but
also because, as Thoreau has it, God's love produces an
impenetrable "heat of heat." This is the point to the
second part of the quotation: Deus est Lumen Luminis
(God is the light of light).[13]

Thomas Taylor, the classicist whose essays and
translations became standard reading material for the
transcendentalists, offered an interpretation of "The
Platonic Philosopher's Creed" that must have influenced
Thoreau in that both conceptually and linguistically it
mirrors the Lumen quotation:

> I believe in one first cause of all
> things, whose nature is so immensely
> transcendent, that it is even
> superessential; and that in
> consequence of this it cannot
> properly either be named, or spoken
> of, or conceived by opinion, or be
> known, or perceived by any being. I
> believe, however, that if it be
> lawful to give a name to that which
> is truly ineffable, the apellations
> of the one and the good are of all
> others the most adapted to it; the

former of these names indicating
that it is the principle of all
things, and the latter that it is
the ultimate object of desire to all
things. I believe that this immense
principle produced such things as
are first and proximate to itself,
most similar to itself; just as the
heat immediately proceeding from
fire is most similar to the heat in
the fire; and the light immediately
emanating from the sun, to that
which the sun essentially contains.[14]

Those who criticize Thoreau's religiosity as being
vague[15] might consider that, on neoplatonic grounds,
Thoreau is doing the best he can with the recalcitrant
subject matter he has to deal with. God-talk in one
sense is shadowy by its very nature. There are clear
neoplatonic reasons why discourse about the divine must
be unclear. If the shadows become bothersome, only two
alternatives remain. One can find "solace" in some
secluded cave, void of light altogether. Or one can fly

like Icarus to the source of light itself.
Unfortunately, as Thoreau realized, this latter course
leaves one blinded and burned.

Added support for my sort of approach can be found
in Thoreau:

> Pythagoras says, truly enough, A
> true assertion respecting God, is an
> assertion of God; but we may well
> doubt if there is any example of
> this in literature.[16]

Regarding merchants, however, whom Thoreau views as
contemporary cavemen in the Platonic sense, he says:

> You grov'ling worldlings, you whose wisdom
> trades/Where light ne'er shot his golden
> ray.[17]

It seems that for Thoreau one can neither live with, nor
without, talk about God.

> Every man casts a shadow...it falls
> opposite to the sun....The divine
> light is diffused almost entirely
> around us....Shadows, referred to
> the source of light, are pyramids

> whose bases are never greater than
> those of the substances which cast
> them.[18]
>
> The right Reason is in part divine,
> in part human; the second can be
> expressed, but no language can
> translate the first.[19]

In this last quotation Thoreau shows a reliance on
Empedocles, who, like Pythagoras but to a lesser degree,
influenced Plato. One final quotation on this theme is
needed:

> But the sun indifferently selects
> his rhymes, and with a liberal taste
> weaves into his verse the planet and
> the stubble. Let us know and
> conform only to the fashions of
> eternity.[20]

Thoreau realized how subtle Plato's philosophy was.
For Thoreau, Plato was a seer who saw more than
himself,[21] such that the bottom of his thought could not
be fathomed.[22] Nonetheless, all of us have what Plato
might call:

...a certain divination, presage,

and parturient vaticination in our

minds, of some higher good and

perfection than either power or

knowledge.[23]

A Platonist is always a lover. In the Symposium
Plato develops, in Socrates' speech, the theory that
love is neither divine nor human, but an intermediary
between the two. Love is a guiding daemon which links
us to the divine, because it is only those who love
wisdom who can possibly find it. The very need to love,
however, indicates that one is somewhat removed from the
object of one's desire. Philosophy itself was conceived
in the Socratic-Platonic tradition as a philia of
sophia, a love of wisdom rather than a necessary
possession of it. Thoreau knew that philia could be
translated in English either as "love" or "friendship,"
and in his treatment of friendship[24] he relies not only
on the Symposium but on Plato's myth of Atlantis as
well.[25] Amidst all of the exotic speculation as to the
possible location of Atlantis, few seriously study the
fact that Plato was the originator of the myth of
Atlantis,[26] a myth which concerns the story of two
ancient powers--Atlantis and ancient Athens. These

powers supposedly existed nine thousand years before
Plato in a nearly utopian condition far superior to that
which Plato's contemporary Athens enjoyed.

In Thoreau's hands in A Week on the Concord and
Merrimack Rivers, Atlantis becomes a symbol for that
sort of being (human or divine) most worthy of our own
philia--a being worthy of a mutinous and stormy voyage
over the Atlantic that will take us to the "fabulous
retreating shores" of the object of true friendship.
Human beings are islands which, although they are sur-
rounded by an ocean of love, have not yet seen the
fabled shores of their completion. Plato's ancient map
contains "some dotted outline of our main," but all we
have now is a mirage of "Ye rumored but untrodden
shore." We are "no nearer than Plato was." Yet as
Wordsworth, another Platonist, had it: what having
been, must ever be. The golden age of Atlantis is
preserved, in however faint an expression, wherever
there is goodness, or love of goodness: "The coming in
of spring is like the creation of Cosmos out of Chaos
and the realization of the Golden Age."[27] The same can
be said about that "laboring gale"[28] and the sapling.[29]
The golden state "before the fall" is also preserved, in

a way, in the principles defended by Socrates in Plato's
Republic, which is governed, as Thoreau sees it, by
love.[30]

Love of perfection presupposes love of life, for
without the latter the former could not be pursued.
Thoreau's love of life was not necessarily restricted to
human life, as the "Higher Laws" to respect animal life
indicate.  His vegetarianism, as we will see in Chapter
Four, is built firmly on the neoplatonic base provided
by Porphyry's De abstinentia, translated by Thomas
Taylor as Abstinence from Animal Food.[31]  To inflict
unnecessary suffering is cruel, and because it is not
necessary to eat meat to maintain a healthy body, eating
meat or fish is cruel.  Anderson supposes that there was
a dilemma Thoreau faced with regard to nature:  either
natural objects really existed "out there" in the world
and thus deserved respect, or natural objects were only
symbols of a higher reality.[32]  But this is a false
dilemma in that natural objects can be both real and
symbolic.  For example, a mirage is an illusionary
symbol of refreshment, but an animal, for Thoreau, as we
will see, is a real, sentient, existent symbol of the
divine.  Thoreau's higher laws regarding animals show

that he believed animals had a concrete status in the
world. But he also says, regarding his "idea" of a
fish, rather than a concrete fish, that:

> I see it for what it is--not an
> actual terrene fish, but the fair
> symbol of a divine idea, the design
> of an artist.[33]

Thoreau's respect for nature is well known, and it
is against the background of this respect that his
attitude toward immortality is to be understood. That
is, Thoreau's views on the afterlife owe more to
classical or Oriental sources than to Christian ones.[34]
He notes[35] that the Athenians believed not only in life
after death, but also that they had sprung from some
previous sort of existence in the earth. A golden
grasshopper was the Athenian emblem which symbolized,
Thoreau implies, a human being's unity with the earth,
and also symbolized continuity and immortality.[36] Plato
might have considered this back-reaching tendency of the
human mind as well, although Thoreau is by no means sure
about this (in fact, Plato did consider it).[37] In any
event, Thoreau informs us that he has no "quarrel" with
belief in immortality. Nor would Plato.[38]

The similarities to Plato's theories regarding immortality are quite specific. The first of three arguments for immortality in the Phaedo (70D) states that opposites generate each other: the dead come from the living and the living come from the dead. As Thoreau illustrates this argument:

> Every one has heard the story which
> has gone the rounds of New England
> of a strong and beautiful bug which
> came out of a dry leaf of an old
> table of apple-tree wood, which had
> stood in a farmer's kitchen for
> sixty years, first in Connecticut,
> and afterwards in Massachusetts,--
> from an egg deposited in the living
> tree many years earlier still, as
> appeared by counting the annual
> layers beyond it; which was heard
> gnawing out for several weeks,
> hatched perchance by the heat of the
> urn. Who does not feel his faith in
> a resurrection and immortality
> strengthened by hearing of this?[39]

At another point he talks about his brother:

> I do not want to see John ever
> again--I mean him who is dead--but
> that other whom only he would have
> wished to see, or to be, of whom he
> was the imperfect representative.
> For we are not what we are, nor do
> we treat or esteem each other for
> such, but for what we are capable of
> being.[40]

As before, however, none of this should be interpreted
as an unbridgable dualism between the eternal and the
temporal in Thoreau's thought because, as in the
Platonic or Johannine traditions, immortality is in a
way present now.  Thoreau can think of no better remedy
for myopia than to read Greek philosophy.[41]

Despite the fact that Thoreau said to Edmund Hosmer
shortly before his own death:  "This is a beautiful
world; but I shall see a fairer,"[42] there is no strict
demarcation between the present and the eternal in that
the former mirrors, albiet in a cloudy way, the
latter.[43]  The following remark that Thoreau made after
his brother's death balances the above quotation:

> My soul and body have tottered along
> together of late, tripping and
> hampering one another like
> unpracticed Siamese twins (my
> emphasis).[44]

The kinship between soul and body is analogous to the relationship between human beings and nature. Thoreau asks whether the "face" of nature would be "so serene if man's destiny were not equally so?" He once got in trouble with an editor for speculating about the immortality of trees.[45]

Thoreau quite bluntly tells us to "waste no time at funerals."[46] And Adams tells us with equal bluntness that Thoreau was a Platonist with respect to immortality, intimations of which are found in sleep.[47] However, Adams and Wolf disagree as to whether Thoreau believed literally in the transmigration of souls from body to body. The former thinks that only eventually does there occur "the final migration of souls out of nature to a serener summer."[48] He notes that Thoreau declares that "We have hardly entered the vestibule of nature."[49] Wolf favors the interpretation, more consonant with Plato's myths of transmigration and metempsychosis, that Thoreau's treatment of

transmigration is a "flight of imagination."[50] Both
would agree that Thoreau, as a good Platonist and
romantic, would affirm:   "Heaven lies about us long
after our infancy."[51]

It should now be obvious that Thoreau did not live
just in an empyrean world of thoughts about, and love
for, eternity, the golden age, and immortality.  As the
two glances passage indicates, as a Platonist he was
also a citizen of "this" world, whose beauty primarily
consists in its ability to accurately mirror essential
reality, even if this world has intrinsic value as well:

> I am not without hope that we may,
>
> even here and now, obtain some
>
> accurate information concerning that
>
> Other World.[52]

Unfortunately, inaccurate mirroring is also possible,
even in Thoreau's beloved Concord.  The citizens there
are like those described by Glaucon in Book Two of the
Republic: they live in community not out of love for
each other, but for mutual defense.[53]  Concord is as
dark as Plato's cave, but at least it provides a
contrast so as to put Thoreau's admiration for Plato in
sharp relief, as indicated in the passage from Walden
dealing with Plato's dialogues, treated in Chapter One.

In this passage, the "I" who never reads Plato obviously
does not refer to Thoreau himself throughout his career,
for he was not the sort who would be content as a "tit-
man" reading only "Connecticut philosophy."[54]

One should not get the impression that Thoreau took
his Platonism too seriously, nor that he necessarily
held his non-Platonic fellows in contempt.  I have
previously noticed that for Thoreau all have a certain
divination, a desire for goodness, and a potential for
wisdom, as the following story about an uneducated
Canadian woodsman indicates:

> He could defend many institutions
> better than any philosopher,
> because, in describing them as they
> concerned him, he gave the true
> reason for their prevalence, and
> speculation had not suggested to him
> any other.  At another time, hearing
> Plato's definition of a man--a biped
> without feathers,--and that one
> exhibited a cock plucked and called
> it Plato's man, he thought it an
> important difference that the knees
> bent the wrong way.[55]

Socrates, more so than Plato, is Thoreau's model in the world of everyday affairs. Thoreau, like Socrates, was a "commoner" who saw "manners" as devilish.[56] Rather than denigrating the material world, however, as some ascetics might do, Thoreau tried to accept it as an image of eternity. He prefers the calm wisdom, or love of it, in Socrates to the enthusiasm of the Delphic priestess.[57] What Thoreau aims for is the "serene countenance" of Socrates in the midst of the inadequate images of eternity, images which the material world sometimes, but only sometimes, brutally offers.[58] The danger in this stoic (or Ignatian) indifference is that one may too passively accept whatever the material world of sicknesses and states offers, without trying to ameliorate the blemishes in that world,[59] because one's destiny is believed to lie in the "other" world. But to succumb to this danger would be to violate the spirit of the two glances passage.

One must look to "this" world as well; we must re-enter the cave, not with a pompous noblesse oblige, but with the humility that comes from the realization that this cave of a world must also be made into a cozy home. We live in our bodies, a belief which Socrates always exhibited, except just before his death in the Phaedo, when his body seemed of little use. Plato himself was a great wrestler; Socrates' mother was a midwife, a profession which he imitated in the Theaetetus. In their own peculiar ways, were not Socrates and Thoreau more at home in the world than anyone else? Think of Socrates' joy in simple conversation, or Thoreau's fascination with the daily routine of ants. Their love for this world led them to risk all to better it. Both were civilly disobedient,[60] again, not so much to divorce themselves from the world, but to grind the Mexican Wars in it to obscurity. Althouth Thoreau did not die for his beliefs, as Socrates did, we suspect that he would have if put to the test. Yet Socrates was uncomfortable with any encomium dedicated to him,[61] and Thoreau realized that what we ought to learn from Socrates is that "a better than Socrates speaks through us every hour."[62] No doubt Socrates would agree, in that his philosophical midwifery consisted in the assistance he gave to others in the birth of their ideas.

The similarity between Thoreau and Socrates becomes most evident when civil disobedience is considered. Civil disobedience is at least as old as Socrates, but in American thought the tradition of civil disobedience has always been traced back to Thoreau. In fact, the very phrase "Civil Disobedience" was first used as a title to Thoreau's now famous essay, which was originally delivered as a lecture under the title "On the Relation of the Individual to the State." The richness of Thoreau's treatment of civil disobedience is evidenced by the fact that whenever a position is taken as regards the legitimacy and limits of civil disobedience, Thoreau's name appears. This is somewhat odd because it is not <u>exactly</u> clear what Thoreau's position on civil disobedience is.

The writings of John Rawls can be used to pinpoint the precise nature of the problem. Rawls notices that the theory of civil disobedience implied in Thoreau's essay is a general one that encompasses two more specific sub-theories. What makes this situation problematic is that Thoreau speaks as if only one theory is involved, all woven of the same cloth. The confusion is multiplied when one realizes that one of these more specific sub-theories is often called a theory of "civil disobedience" as well. For purposes of clarity, the following diagram will help in a heuristic way as a road map to help us understand Thoreau better:

CIVIL DISOBEDIENCE (G)

CIVIL DISOBEDIENCE (S)          CONSCIENTIOUS REFUSAL

The general use of the phrase "civil disobedience" (G) refers to Thoreau's own general treatment of civil disobedience, which has become the traditional illustration of what civil disobedience is. The specific use of the phrase "civil disobedience" (S) and the phrase "conscientious refusal" refer to Rawls's designations, which are meant to clarify Thoreau's essay, among other things. What Rawls notices is that civil disobedience (G) can mean either civil disobedience (S) or conscientious refusal, or both civil disobedience (S) and conscientious refusal.

Civil disobedience (S) refers to public, nonviolent acts of breaking the law. These acts are done with the aim of bringing about change in a law that permits injustices to be enacted against citizens in a democratic form of government. Since the aim of civil disobedience (S) is to change the law in a democracy, civil disobedience (S) succeeds only if (when it addresses the sense of justice of the majority) the consciences of the perpetrators of the injustice are raised. Examples of successful civil disobedence (S) include the sit-ins organized by Martin Luther King in the 1960s, which were meant to appeal to the sense of justice of the American people, and Gandhi's efforts to gain independence for India in the 1940s, efforts which were intended to appeal to Britain's sense of humanity (and Gandhi, along with King, was a follower of both Socrates and Thoreau).

By way of contrast, conscientious refusal refers to noncompliance with the law for reasons of conscience (or religion). Therefore, conscientious refusal is not done with the aim (or even the hope, in some instances) of changing the law. However, if unjust laws were changed for the better the conscientious refuser would not object. Nor would the conscientious refuser seek occasions for disobedience as a way to state one's cause, as does the civilly disobedient (S) person. Rather, the conscientious refuser hopes those situations that test one's conscience do not occur. The person who conscientiously refuses to obey certain dictates of the state would refuse even if one's efforts were not efficacious in changing the will of the majority. Conscientious refusal concerns matters of principle, without regard for utilitarian concerns. Examples include the refusal of the early Christians to perform certain acts of pagan piety and the refusal of pacifists to engage in war, even a "popular" war such as World War Two, in which there was little, if any, hope of winning adherents to pacifism.

With this Rawlsian distinction between civil disobedience (S) and conscientious refusal as a background, we have these key questions: was Thoreau's essay a justification of civil disobedience (S) or conscientious refusal or both? And how does Thoreau resemble Socrates? Answers to these questions are of the utmost importance for understanding Thoreau's thought.

Thoreau wrote his essay in reference to his refusal to pay the poll tax in Massachusetts, which caused him to suffer a night in jail. Since he disobeyed the tax laws on the grounds that to obey them would make him an agent of grave injustice to other persons (because of the Mexican War, slavery) it seems that Thoreau is primarily justifying his actions on grounds of conscientious refusal. In other words, regardless of whether his actions would change the conscience of the majority he would refuse to pay the poll tax. We are reminded here of Socrates' claim in the Apology that if freed he would continue to practice philosophy as before. Thoreau notes that to wait until the majority felt as he did would "take too much time, and a man's life will be gone." Also, Thoreau's chastisement of the utilitarian defense of the law offered by Paley shows that Thoreau is primarily concerned with conscientious refusal.

Rawls, however, seems to overstate his case when he suggests that Thoreau is <u>exclusively</u> concerned with conscientious refusal. There is evidence which suggests that Thoreau is concerned in a <u>secondary</u> way with civil disobedience (S). Despite the recalcitrance of his neighbors, Thoreau says: "I am doing my part to educate my fellow-countrymen now." Because this essay was first presented in 1848, two years after Thoreau's jail sentence, it is not clear whether this "now" refers only to his essay on civil disobedience or to his civilly disobedient acts as well. Although Thoreau does not think that this education will be accomplished in his own lifetime, he does have some hope that eventually the majority will realize the individual is a higher power than the state. To this extent, at least, Thoreau is addressing himself to the conscience (or better, the individual consciences) of the majority, and justifying civil disobedience (S). It should also be remembered that Socrates thought of himself as a gadfly to Athens.

In short, the generality of Thoreau's notion of civil disobedience is clarified by Rawls's distinction between two distinct entities: civil disobedience (S) and conscientious refusal. This clarification shows that Thoreau's primary intent in his essay is to justify the latter, but not to the exclusion of the former. It is part of Thoreau's genius that he, like Socrates, can have his cake and eat it too, a feat that has seldom been repeated by those who are civilly disobedient or those who are conscientious refusers.

It should now be clear that Thoreau was interested in both eternity and the temporal world. How else was he Platonic? William Howarth suggests that a "Platonic bias" colored Thoreau's early years in that he believed the mind shapes reality.[63] But this sounds more Hegelian than Platonic. Thoreau's mind does not create the eternal world, but the other way around. "Let us know and conform only to the fashions of eternity" (my emphasis).[64] Howarth is on safer ground when he notices Thoreau's allusion to Plato's allegory of the cave: the mind can see the substance of objective reality even if the bliss of cavelike ignorance is hard to part with.[65] Although one might not make this cave of a world a significantly better place in one's own lifetime, as

Thoreau did not, we should remember the advice of Henry Salt that says "the unaccomplished aspirations of a man also have to be taken into account in an estimate of him."[66] Nonetheless, Salt would oppose the definition of the philosopher as one whose family and friends must hold the ropes on his philosophical balloon to prevent him from floating off into the Aristophanes-like clouds.[67] Wolf agrees that Thoreau was not a rigid "Platonic dualist" trying to fly off into another world, but was even Plato ever a rigid Platonic dualist? Certainly there is not evidence of this in his earlier or later dialogues, probably not in his middle dialogues either. Thoreau rightly reminds us that:

> Even here we have a sort of living
> to get, and must buffet it somewhat
> longer. There are various tough
> problems yet to solve, and we must
> make shift to live, betwixt spirit
> and matter, such a human life as we
> can.[68]

The following quotation even more accurately mirrors the two glances passage:

> I found in myself, and still find,
>
> an instinct toward a higher, or, as
>
> it is named, spiritual life, as do
>
> most men, and another toward a
>
> primitive rank and savage one, and I
>
> reverence them both.[69]

Likewise, one of the most important features of
Plato's Republic is the parallel between the individual
and the state, on the one hand, and between both of
these and the universe, on the other. The just
individual or state is the one which can legislate the
proper harmony for its parts. Thoreau's political beliefs are well known, and would indicate that he did not
see harmony in the state, hence little justice. Yet
America had freed itself from at least one form of
colonial tyranny, leaving Americans enslaved to their
moral and economic selfishness. As he put it:

> Now that the republic--the res
>
> publica--has been settled, it is
>
> time to look after the res privata-
>
> -the private state.[70]

An atomic anthropology inevitably leads to cacophany,
Thoreau seems to hold. Much more to his liking is that
individualism constituitive of true cosmopolitanism, a

cosmopolitanism which consists in the realization that
we can "pass at last from the farthest brink of time to
the nearest shore of eternity!"[71] The best individuals
he knows are those who dwell in forms,[72] and it does not
seem too bold to suggest that he means Platonic Forms,
wherein reside "eternal justice and glory."[73] The most
accurate imitation of the harmony among the eternal
Forms is found in music, concerning which Thoreau notes
the following:

> Plato thinks the gods never gave men
> music, the science of melody and
> harmony, for mere delectation or to
> tickle the ear; but that the
> discordant parts of the circulations
> and beauteous fabric of the soul,
> and that of it that roves about the
> body, and many times, for want of
> tune and air, breaks forth into many
> extravagences and excesses, might be
> sweetly recalled and artfully wound
> up to their former consent and
> agreement.[74]

The obstacles to harmony are twofold. First, harmony of soul or state can be prevented by a myopia that focuses on some particular part of the cosmos at the expense of some other part; that is, by allowing one's glance to turn into a dull, often self-centered, mirror-imaged stare. To prevent this, Thoreau encourages us to balance our vision of time and eternity. He notices that Carlyle's works are defective in that they concentrate only on men of action and not on poets, saints, or philosophers like Plato:

> ...whose kingdoms are wholly in the hearts of their subjects, strictly transcendent.[75]

These two, practicality and contemplation, are complementary for Thoreau, in the way that Aristotle and Plato, respectively, are complementary. However, Aristotle and Plato shared each other's characteristics.[76] Thoreau's writings are full of warnings regarding the more likely danger in his not so New England: that science, the desire for profit, and the like would pull us down to earth too often, and too superficially. If he is to err it will be in the other

direction as compensation for his fellows. Thoreau
tells us explicitly that his "science" is quite like
Plato's:

> The fact is I am a mystic, a
> transcendentalist, and a natural
> philosopher to boot.[77]

Yet wisdom for Thoreau was supremely practical in that
it taught one how to live. The following series of
rhetorical questions gives us an indication of Thoreau's
position:

> How can a man be a wise man, if he
> doesn't know any better how to live
> than other men? --if he is only more
> cunning and intellectually subtle?
> Does Wisdom fail? or does she teach
> how to succeed by her example? Is
> she merely the miller who grinds the
> finest logic? Did Plato get his
> living in a better way or more
> successfully than his contempo-
> raries? Did he succumb to the
> difficulties of life like other men?
> Did he merely prevail over them by
> indifference, or by assuming grand

airs?  or find it easier to live

because his aunt remembered him in

her will?[78]

The last question alludes to death, which leads us to
the second great obstacle to harmony:  fate.  Relying on
the myth of Er in Book Ten of the Republic,[79] Thoreau
realizes that we are often shaken by disease, death, and
other still contemporary fates beyond our control and
beyond divine control.  Socratic and Platonic wisdom,
however, indicates to him that although all things are
within the sphere of fate, not all particular events are
fated:

It is not in fate that one man shall

do so and so, and another suffer so

and so, for that would be the

destruction of our free agency and

liberty:  but if any one should

choose such a life, and do such or

such things, then it is in fate that

such or such consequences shall

ensue upon it.[80]

We are fated to live with our free choices, including
our choice regarding how we will think about death.
Only those who realize this are capable of hearing,
along with Plato's forerunner Pythagoras and his
follower Iamblichus, the:

> ...sublime symphonies of the world,
> he alone (Pythagoras) hearing and
> understanding, as it appears, the
> universal harmony and consonance of
> the spheres.[81]

To hear these symphonies is not only difficult, but also
a terribly lonely endeavor in a cacophonous world of
idle chatter:

> Then idle Time ran gadding by and
> left me in the Eternity alone; I
> hear beyond the range of sound, I
> see beyond the verge of sight.[82]

This seeing "beyond the verge of sight" reminds us again
of:

> ...the sun, that old Platonist,
> (which) is set so far off in the
> heavens, that only a genial summer-
> heat and ineffable day-light can
> reach us.[83]

But in wintery weather, when the sun cannot be found at all, one can rest content with the "Promethean flames" of a mere Carlyle.[84]

To "know thyself" was the motto of several Greek philosophers, especially Socrates. Thoreau does his best to gain such knowledge, and at those moments when he is forced into agnosticism about himself he at least can tell a likely story, like Plato's use of bastard reason in the _Timaeus_, which imitates true knowledge: "know what thou canst work at."[85] This less exalted ideal should not confuse us into thinking that Thoreau was not enamored of (Platonic) philosophy. Even if philosophy does not give us _the_ truth in minute detail about the human person, it at least gives us an attitude[86] or a structure within which we can either find or discuss truth. Yet:

> To live like a philosopher, is to
> live, not foolishly, like other men,
> but wisely, and according to
> universal laws. In this which was
> the ancient sense, we think there
> has been no philosopher in modern
> times.[87]

Thoreau makes no ultimate distinctions between the poet
and the philosopher; the former generalizes on the
deductions of the latter. Both reflect the rays of the
sun (again, a symbol of the Form of the Good or the
source-ground for knowledge) like clouds, but not to
such an extent that these rays cannot be blinding. The
philosophic or poetic seers--Plato among them, as we
have seen--keep their eyes on the true and real, however
difficult this may be. It is because the philosophic
life is so demanding that philosophers should live
simply. Thoreau is surprised that in France and Germany
some philosophers receive a considerable salary. Today
there are only professors of philosophy, he thinks,
readers and speakers of it only. To be a philosopher
one must lead a life of simplicity, magnanimity, and
trust. Herein lies Thoreau's admiration for the ancient
philosophers who embodied wisdom. Richest in inward
riches, poorest in outward riches, these philosophers
have been confused by some with Oriental sages. Indeed
at times Thoreau favorably compares the Stoics with the
Brahmins. But his overall view seems to be that the
Greek thinkers avoid the purely contemplative wisdom of
the Orient in favor of a life mixed with practical
affairs, just as Plato argues in favor of the mixed life

in the Philebus. To recapture the Greek philosophic
spirit it seems we must, before all else, slow down the
frenzied pace of modern life; we must learn once again
to read and speak with care so that we can act with
care. Speaking of Pythagoras, Iamblichus, and Plato, he
says, as we have seen Channing notice, that:

> Their long stringy slimy sentences
> are of that consistency that they
> naturally flow and run
> together....They are slower than a
> Roman army in its march, the rear
> camping tonight where the van camped
> last night.[88]

If we were to slow down in a Thoreauvian way--yet
working all the while, so as to improve the nick of
time--we might come to see Plato not only as sincere but
also as "irresistable."[89]

Reading Plato, for Thoreau, is reading well,[90] and
although Plato is a dead philosopher, the material world
provides imaged evidence of the ideal world he talked
about, but only through the mediation of the human
beings who bridge these two worlds. We can see that the
wood thrush, a more modern "philosopher" than Plato,
preaches the doctrine of this hour.[91] In the final

analysis, Thoreau's Platonism must be seen as similar to that of Whitehead,[92] in which at the heart of things there are always the formal dream of youth and the material harvest of tragedy. Thoreau's adventure was to keep the dream alive, even if what we dream about does not need our adventure; to keep this dream alive while tragedy is reaped. In this way he tries to persuade us toward such perfections as are possible in this world.

Joseph Millichap has done more to call attention to the relationship between Thoreau and Plato than any other scholar, but he restricts his analysis to Plato's allegory of the cave. This is not a bad choice. Thoreau himself notices that many people have dated a new era in their lives from the reading of a book; Millichap thinks it probable (not just possible) that Plato's dialogues had such an effect on Thoreau.[93] What Thoreau learned from Plato's allegory of the cave in the Republic is that shams and delusions are taken as soundest truths while reality appears fabulous. But the chains on the prisoners in the cave are self-imposed; people consent to be deceived by shows. Thoreau's solace comes in the hope that just as the insect worked its way out of the table after such a long period of dormancy, so might contemporary "cavemen" go through a

spiritual metamorphosis. Materially, however, many
people have evolved too far from the cave, which offered
simple shelter.[94] That is, the suburban box and the
urban condo become elaborate traps. Also the com-
modified farm or vacation "getaway."

# NOTES: CHAPTER TWO

[1]See Plato's Sophist (249D).

[2]A Week on the Concord and Merrimack Rivers, ed. by Hovde, Howarth, Witherell (Princeton: Princeton University Press, 1980), p. 386.

[3]Ibid.

[4]Walden, p. 8. Also see Journal, volume 1, ed. by Witherell, Howarth, Sattelmeyer, Blanding (Princeton: Princeton University Press, 1981), p. 185. "What is sacrificed to time is lost to eternity." Plato's famous treatment of time as a moving image of eternity is found in the Timaeus (37D).

[5]Walden, p. 17.

[6]Journal, volume 1, p. 280.

[7]See "Sir Walter Raleigh," in Early Essays and Miscellanies, ed. by Moldenhauer, Moser, Kern (Princeton: Princeton University Press, 1975), p. 204. And "Paradise (to be) Regained," in Reform Papers, ed. by Glick (Princeton: Princeton University Press, 1973), pp. 46-47. Also see my "Lumen est umbra Dei, Deus est Lumen Luminis," The Clasical Bulletin 60 (Spring, 1984), pp. 28-29.

[8]Republic (507B-509D). Also see the subsequent divided line and allegory of the cave passages. Cameron, Transcendental Apprenticeship, pp. 218-220,

makes it clear that Thoreau was aware in this quotation
of Plotinus' influence on Raleigh.

[9]See J. Prescott Johnson, "The Ontological Argument
in Plato," Personalist (Winter, 1963), pp. 24-34, for
the best treatment of why The Good is needed.

[10]One of the key differences between dianoia and
noesis (noesis being the highest type of episteme--
knowledge) is the inabilty of dianoia to establish its
own premises in a non-hypothetical way.

[11]In fact, there is considerable evidence that
Plato later abandoned his belief in an "absolute one,"
i.e., The Good. See my Plato's Philosophy of History
(Washington, D.C.: University Press of America, 1981),
Chapter Six. Also a review of this book by Charles
Hartshorne, Process Studies 12 (1982), pp. 201-202.

[12]See, for example, his Enneads III.8; V.1-6;
VI.7-9.

[13]Walter Harding admits that among the
transcendentalists Thoreau was the most proficient in
the classics. See his The Variorum Walden (New York:
Twayne, 1962), p. 286, note 3. Thoreau's subtle ability
to massage the texts of Plotinus (and Raleigh) here is
evidence of Harding's point.

[14]Taylor's essay was first published in 1805, and

can be found in Kathleen Raine and George Mills Harper,
eds., Thomas Taylor the Platonist (Princeton: Princeton
University Press, 1969), p. 439. Harper's introduction
to this volume details the important influence Taylor
had on the transcendentalist movement. Compare
especially the heat metaphor in Taylor with Thoreau's
comments on the text from Raleigh.

[15]There is a long history to such criticism. One
recent author who sees Thoreau's religiosity as not only
vague but dangerous is Laraine Fergenson, "Thoreau,
Daniel Berrigan, and the Problem of Transcendental
Politics," Soundings (Spring, 1982), pp. 103-122.

[16]A Week, p. 71.

[17]Ibid., p. 97.

[18]Ibid., pp. 352-353.

[19]Journal, volume 1, p. 127.

[20]Ibid., p. 326.

[21]The Writings of Henry David Thoreau (New York:
AMS Press, 1968), reprinted from the 1906 edition, 6, p.
150. Millichap, p. 277, quotes Thoreau's Journal to the
effect that Plato "...Takes me up into the serene
heavens and paints earth and sky."

[22]Early Essays, p. 52.

[23]Writings, 8, p. 150. This divination is called

manteuma te in Greek. Also see Stanley Cavell, The
Senses of Walden (San Francisco: North Point, 1981), p.
87, where the author sees Thoreau's society in New
England as a prison. The path out of this prison is as
arduous as that out of Plato's cave into the light of
the sun, which presides over Thoreau's world in Walden.
Cavell's book was originally published in 1972 by Viking
Press.

[24]A Week, pp. 261-263. Also see Wolf, pp. 71-72,
who notices that Thoreau's treatment of friendship in A
Week relies on the subtle difference between Plato's
eros and philia, and also between these two and
Christian agape.

[25]See Plato's Timaeus (17-27) and the unfinished
Critias.

[26]See my "Atlantis and Plato's Philosophy," Apeiron
XV (1981), pp. 117-128, for a detailed interpretation of
the function this myth plays in Plato's philosophy.

[27]Walden, pp. 313-314. Thoreau's notion of
creation is that of an "Artificer" creating order out of
disorderly, chaotic matter, but not creating this chaos
itself. This is much closer to Plato's myth of creation
in the Timaeus than to the Judeo-Christian belief in
creation ex nihilo. For Plato's myth see Timaeus (27

ff.), the same dialogue in which the myth of Atlantis is introduced.

[28]A Week, p. 164.

[29]Journal, volume 1, p. 216.

[30]Writings, 7, p. 121. Also see Early Essays, p. 258. Plato's Republic is the scene of love just as paradise belonged to Adam and Eve. See Journal, volume 2, p. 6.

[31]That Thoreau read this work is shown by Seybold, pp. 15, 41. See my articles on "Thoreau, Sainthood, and Vegetarianism," forthcoming in The American Transcendental Quarterly; "Vegetarianism and the Argument from Marginal Cases in Porphyry," Journal of the History of Ideas XLV (March, 1984), pp. 141-143; and "Was Plato a Vegetarian?," Apeiron XVIII (June, 1984), pp. 1-9. Also see my The Philosophy of Vegetarianism (Amherst: University of Massachusetts Press, 1984).

[32]Anderson, p. 93.

[33]Writings, 9, pp. 437-438.

[34]Writings, 6, p. 113, where Thoreau contrasts the saintliness of some Christian order with devotion to Plato.

[35]Journal, volume 1, p. 412.

[36]Seybold, p. 30. Plato also uses the myth of

earthborn men several times: Menexenus (237B), Critias (113C), Statesman (269 ff.). Also see A Week, p. 380, where Thoreau even says that we need to be earthborn (geneneis). And Journal, volume 2, pp. 55.

[37]Contrast Journal, volume 1, p. 412, with Writings, 7, p. 19. Also see the theory (or myth?) of recollection (anamnesis) in Plato's Meno or Wordsworth's "Intimations of Immortality."

[38]See the famous arguments for the immortality of the soul in the Phaedo.

[39]Walden, p. 333.

[40]See Walter Harding and Carl Bode, eds., The Correspondence of Henry David Thoreau (New York: New York University Press, 1958), p. 62.

[41]See Writings, 7, pp. 187-188. Also Journal, volume 2, p. 201.

[42]Quoted in Adams, p. 58.

[43]Ibid., p. 59, where Adams makes this point.

[44]Ibid., p. 60, where Adams quotes from Thoreau's Journal.

[45]Ibid., p. 61.

[46]Ibid., where Adams quotes from a loose manuscript written by Thoreau.

[47]Ibid., p. 62.

[48]Ibid., p. 64. Adams relies primarliy on Thoreau's _Journal_ in the development of his thesis regarding Thoreau's belief in transmigration.

[49]Ibid., p. 65, from Thoreau's _Journal_.

[50]Wolf, p. 142.

[51]See Adams, p. 66.

[52]_A Week_, p. 385.

[53]_Walden_, p. 153.

[54]The passage from _Walden_ treated in Chapter One is found on p. 107. Also see _Writings_, 6, p. 146.

[55]_Walden_, p. 149.

[56]_Writings_, 9, p. 256. Also see an anonymous 1857 British criticism of Thoreau titled "An American Diogenes," in Walter Harding, ed., _Thoreau: A Century of Criticism_ (Dallas: Southern Methodist University Press, 1965).

[57]_A Week_, p. 128.

[58]_Journal_, volume 1, p. 396.

[59]_A Week_, p. 132.

[60]Consider, for example, the trouble Socrates received for refusing to arrest a man because it was unfair in this particular instance to arrest the man. Also see my "Rawls and Thoreau on Civil Disobedience," _Thoreau Journal Quarterly_ XI (1979), pp. 55-58. Seybold

seems to think that Thoreau tried to better the world around him because he was shut out from the world of ideal beauty. She seems to misunderstand the "two glances" character of Thoreau's thought. See Seybold, p. 75. Finally, we should keep in mind Thoreau's conscientious refusal when he was involved in hiding runaway slaves.

[61]See, for example, his response to Alcibiades' speech in the Symposium.

[62]Journal, volume 1, p. 189. In the treatment of civil disobedience that follows I have used the version in Reform Papers. For John Rawls, see his magnum opus A Theory of Justice (Cambridge: Harvard University Press, 1971), pp. 363-371.

[63]William Howarth, The Book of Concord: Thoreau's Life as a Writer (New York: Viking Press, 1982), p. 20.

[64]Journal, volume 1, p. 326.

[65]See Howarth, p. 139, who relies on Thoreau's Journal.

[66]In Fritz Oehlschlaeger and George Hendrick, eds., Toward the Making of Thoreau's Modern Reputation (Urbana: University of Illinois Press, 1979), p. 187. Thoreau himself would agree with Salt: the best way to compare people is to compare their ideals, and this

because concrete individuals are too complex to deal with. See *Journal*, volume 2, p. 222.

[67]Ibid., S.A. Jones, in a letter to Henry Salt, recites this popular definition.

[68]Quoted in Wolf, p. 59; from *A Week*.

[69]Ibid., p. 98; from *Walden*, p. 210.

[70]*Reform Papers*, p. 174.

[71]Ibid., p. 173. This quotation once again alludes to Plato's *Timaeus*.

[72]Ibid., p. 168.

[73]Ibid., p. 147. The fact that Thoreau considered Platonic Forms can be shown when he says that material trees have as their model a perfect exemplar, presumably an immaterial one. See *Journal*, volume 2, p. 11.

[74]*A Week*, p. 175. Also see *Reform Papers*, p. 10. And *Journal*, volume 1, pp. 97, 447.

[75]*Early Essays*, p. 250.

[76]*Writings*, 7, p. 440. Also see Sherman Paul, *The Shores of America* (Urbana: University of Illinois Press, 1958), p. 209, where the author states that Plato himself was partial because he was only a thinker and not a man of action. But this position not only ignores the fact that Plato did not merely teach in but *founded* the first institution of higher learning in Western

culture, which lasted about a thousand years, it also
ignores Plato's practical efforts in Sicily to establish
a philosopher-king there. Plato would not agree with
the Oriental conception of philosophy as "an entire
separation from the world." See Emerson's selections
from the "Veeshnoo Sarma" in The Dial (July, 1842),
reproduced in Cameron, Transcendental Apprenticeship,
pp. 176-177. Finally, see Journal, volume 2, p. 240, on
Thoreau's struggle between love of contemplation and
(heroic) love of action.

[77]Writings, 2, pp. 4-5.

[78]Ibid., 12, pp. 208-209. I think what Thoreau is
trying to get at in these questions is that Plato did no
better job of getting life's necessities than anyone
else, but the fact that he recognized life's necessities
as necessities, and not frivolities as necessities,
gives him distinction. Also see Reform Papers, p. 162,
where Thoreau contrasts Plato with most men: "The ways
in which most men get their living, that is, live, are
mere make-shifts, and a shirking of the real business of
life."

[79]Early Essays, p. 59. Especially see Thoreau's
and Plato's references to the three fates: Clotho,
Lachesis, and Atropos.

[80] Ibid. Thoreau makes it explicit that this is the view of Socrates and Plato. F.B. Sanborn quotes Thoreau as claiming that Plato's views on fate were correct. See The Life of Henry David Thoreau (1917), p. 176.

[81] A Week, p. 176.

[82] Ibid., p. 173.

[83] Early Essays, p. 239.

[84] Ibid.

[85] Ibid., p. 254. Plato's Timaeus and other dialogues written after his disastrous trips to Sicily (and after the criticisms of the Forms in the Parmenides) are full of such likely stories, or in the case of the description of the Receptacle, bastard reasonings.

[86] Journal, volume 1, p. 428.

[87] Early Essays, p. 256. For Thoreau's remarks on ancient philosophy see Journal, volume 2, pp. 53, 144, 145, 220, 355-357, 371, 570.

[88] A Week, p. 103. Also see Writings, 7, p. 150; 7, pp. 352-353; 7, p. 369.

[89] A Week, p. 152.

[90] Writings, 6, p. 153.

[91] Ibid., 7, p. 171.

[92]See, for example, his "Peace" in <u>Adventures of Ideas</u> (New York: Macmillan, 1933).

[93]Millichap, pp. 274-282.

[94]Ibid., p. 281.

## CHAPTER THREE:  THOREAU'S DIPOLAR THEISM

In the previous chapter I emphasized that to understand Thoreau's thought one must notice his two glances. Human beings are sandwiched in between two worlds and must act as mediators or judges in the midst of the claims both worlds make. In this chapter I want to explore Thoreau's thoughts on God in order to show that the two glances are also necessary in Thoreauvian theism: one at divine transcendence and another at divine immanence. I will call Thoreau a dipolar theist for reasons that will become apparent; and I will be relying on the thought of the greatest living dipolar theist, Charles Hartshorne, as well as on the thought of the first great dipolar theist, Plato. I will suggest also why it is plausible to call Thoreau a dipolar theist in spite of himself, in that he never would have used the technical philosophical jargon:  dipolar theism.

Anderson is surely correct in claiming that Thoreau, as a transcendentalist, was strictly obedient to a higher power in the universe, even if he was shy of rational theories about God, even shy of the name "God."[1] Caution must be displayed when putting Thoreau into a category, or when affixing a label to him. But even those Thoreau interpreters who make this point themselves categorize Thoreau and affix labels to him, at least if they are interpreters. The trick is to avoid egregious errors in categorization and to affix labels without dogmatism so that the texts themselves can breathe. To call Thoreau either a pantheist or a believer in a strictly transcendent God is to leave something significant in his thought unexplained. To call him a dipolar theist is to get a little closer, I think, to his thought on God. Yet when dealing with thoughts as rich as those of Thoreau, thoughts too deep for tears, getting a little closer may be going a long way.

What exactly is God for Thoreau? Scholars have given at least two quite different answers. First, there is the view that Thoreau's God was immanent, that is, in the material world. Anderson suggests that Thoreau was "more pan-theist than Christian theist."[2] Perhaps alluding to Jesus' remark that God cares even for the fall of a sparrow,[3] Thoreau himself tells us that the redbird is the first of God.[4] It is remarks like these which induce John Pickard to say that Thoreau had an "ecstatic identification of nature with God" (my emphasis).[5] But Pickard claims also that Thoreau later withdrew from pantheism; unfortunately it is unclear what Pickard thinks was Thoreau's replacement.[6] Horace Greeley and Joseph Krutch also see Thoreau as a pantheist.[7]

The second view emphasizes Thoreau's belief in divine transcendence. Emerson's alleged pantheism was, as Willard Thorpe notices, an obvious influence on Thoreau, but "Nature was to Thoreau a catalyst-- precipitating his love of God."[8] This suggests that God was in some way beyond nature. In what way? The fact that Thoreau disliked the excessively male terms applied to the traditionally omnipotent God[9] indicates that the transcendence of Thoreau's God cannot be assumed to be the transcendence of the traditional Christian God. Anderson, who, as I have noted, claimed Thoreau to be more of a pantheist than a Christian, also notices that God, for Thoreau, is alone, like the sun.[10] This reminds us of the divine transcendence in the Sir Walter Raleigh quotation discussed in Chapter Two, in that neither the sun nor the other stars were believed by many of the ancients to be efficient causes, but rather final causes.[11] Paul Elmer More, who has written one of the most important works on religion in Plato, complicates matters even more by suggesting that there

is hardly a trace of pantheism in Thoreau at all,[12] an
interpretation which in effect balances at the other
extreme the pantheistic interpretations of Thorpe,
Krutch, Greeley, etc. Anderson and Pickard waver
between the two views.

What is religion for Thoreau? That which is never
spoken.[13] That is, Thoreau's mystical states (which are
gold leaf, if not solid gold[14]) must also be accounted
for if the dipolar theistic interpretation of Thoreau is
to hold water. As a heuristic device let me turn to
Hartshorne so as to disentangle what must now seem the
mess of Thoreau's God. Eventually the fruitfulness of
considering Hartshorne will become quite apparent.

Hartshorne fully accepts the goal of traditional
Christian philosophers; that is, logical analysis is in
the service of a higher end.[15] But he holds that the
classical conception of God is internally incoherent.
One of the major complaints Hartshorne has with
classical theism (in philosophy and theology, as opposed
to biblical theism) is that it either explicitly or
implicitly identifies God as active and not passive.
St. Thomas Aquinas' unmoved mover is the most obvious
example of this tendency, but in general classical
theists see God as a timeless, supernatural being that

does not change. The classical theist's inconsistency
lies in his also claiming that God knows and loves. For
example, if God knows, God must be a subject on the
analogy of human subjects, even if divine knowing is
connected with divine willing. And if God is a subject
who knows, God must be affected by, be passive with
respect to, the object known.

It will be to our advantage to get as clear as we
can on what we mean by the term "God." For Hartshorne,
the term refers to the supremely excellent, or all-
worshipful being. Hartshorne has been the most
important defender of the ontological argument for God
in this century, and his debt to St. Anselm is evident
in this preliminary definition.[16] The definition closely
resembles St. Anselm's "that than which no greater can
be conceived." Yet the ontological argument is not what
is at stake here. Even if the argument fails, which
Hartshorne would doubt, the preliminary definition of
God as the supremely excellent being, the all-worshipful
being, or the greatest conceivable being seems un-
objectionable. To say that God can be defined in these
ways still leaves open the possibility that God is even
more excellent or worshipful than we can conceive of.
This allows us to avoid objections from Thomists or

mystics or Thoreau scholars who fear that by defining
God we are limiting God to "merely" human language. All
Hartshorne is suggesting is that when we think of God we
must be thinking of a being that surpasses all others,
or we are not thinking of God. Even the atheist or
agnostic would admit this much. When the atheist says
"There is no God" he is denying that a supremely
excellent, all-worshipful, greatest conceivable being
exists.

The contrast excellent-inferior is the truly
invidious contrast when applied to God. If to be
invidious is to be injurious, then this contrast is the
most invidious one of all when applied (both terms) to
God because God is only excellent. God is inferior in
no way. Period. To suggest that God is in some small
way inferior to some other being is to no longer speak
about God but about some being that is not supremely
excellent, or all-worshipful, or the greatest
conceivable. Hartshorne's major criticism of classical
theism is that its proponents have assumed that all
contrasts, or most of them, when applied to God are
invidious.

Let us assume from now on that God exists. What
attributes does God possess? Consider the following two
columns of attributes in polar contrast to each other:

| | |
|---|---|
| one | many |
| being | becoming |
| activity | passivity |
| permanence | change |
| necessity | contingency |
| self-sufficiency | dependency |
| actuality | potentiality |
| absoluteness | relativity |
| abstractness | concreteness |

Classical theism tends toward oversimplification. It is
comparatively easy to say "God is strong rather than
weak, so in all relations God is active, not passive."
In each case, the classical theist decides which member
of the contrasting pair is good (on the left) and then
attributes it to God, while wholly denying the
contrasting term (on the right). Hence, God is one but
not many, permanent but not changing, etc. This leads
to what Hartshorne calls the monopolar prejudice.
Monopolarity is common to both classical theism and
pantheism, with the major difference between the two
being the fact that classical theism admits the reality

of plurality, potentiality, and becoming as a secondary
form of existence "outside" God (on the right), whereas
in pantheism God includes all reality within itself.
Common to both classical theism and pantheism is the
belief that the above categorial contrasts are
invidious. The dilemma defenders of these two positions
face is that either the deity is only one consitituent
of the whole (classical theism) or else the alleged
inferior pole in each contrast (on the right) is
illusory (pantheism). I will show that Thoreau avoided
both of these positions.

For Hartshorne this dilemma is artificial. It is
produced by the assumption that excellence is found by
separating and purifying one pole (on the left) and
denigrating the other (on the right). That this is not
the case can be seen by analyzing some of the attributes
on the right side. At least since St. Augustine,
classical theists have been convinced that God's
eternity meant not that God endured through all time,
but that God was outside of time altogether and did not,
could not, be receptive to temporal change. St. Thomas
Aquinas identified God, following Aristotle, not Plato,
as unmoved. Yet both activity and passivity can be
either good or bad. Good passivity is likely to be

called sensitivity, responsiveness, adaptability, sympathy, and the like. Insufficiently subtle or defective passivity is called wooden inflexibility, mulish stubborness, inadaptability, unresponsiveness, and the like. Passivity per se refers to the way in which an individual's activity takes account of, and renders itself appropriate to, the activities of others. To deny God passivity altogether is to deny God those aspects of passivity that are excellences. Or again, to altogether deny God the ability to change does avoid fickleness, but at the expense of the ability to lovingly react to the sufferings of others. For Thoreau this is too great a price to pay, as we will see.

The terms on the left side have both good and bad aspects as well. Oneness can mean wholeness, but it can also mean monotony or triviality. Actuality can mean definiteness, but it can mean non-relatedness to others. What happens to divine love when God, according to St. Thomas Aquinas, is claimed to be pure actuality? God ends up loving the world, but is not intrinsically related to it, whatever sort of love that may be. Self-sufficiency can, at times, be selfishness.

The trick when thinking of God, for Hartshorne, is
to attribute to God all excellences (left and right
sides) and not to attribute to God any inferiorities
(right and left sides).  In short, excellent-inferior or
good-evil are invidious contrasts.  Unlike classical
theism and pantheism, Hartshorne's and Thoreau's theism
is dipolar.  To be specific, within each pole of a non-
invidious contrast (for example, permanence-change)
there are invidious elements (inferior permanence or
inferior change), but also non-invidious, good elements
(excellent permanence or excellent change).  Hence,
dipolar theism can also be called the dual
"transcendence" view in that divine permanence and
change are supreme.

Hartshorne does not believe in two gods, one
unified and the other plural, etc.  Rather he believes
that what are often thought to be contraries are really
mutually interdependent correlatives:

> The good as we know it is unity-in-
> variety, or variety-in-unity; if the
> variety overbalances, we have chaos
> or discord; if the unity, we have
> monotony or triviality.[17]

Supreme excellence, if it is truly supreme excellence, must somehow be able to integrate all the complexity there is in the world into itself as one spiritual whole. The word "must" indicates divine necessity, along with God's essence, which is to necessarily exist. And the word "complexity" indicates the contingency that affects God through creaturely decisions or feelings. But in the classical theistic view God is solely identified with the stony immobility of the absolute, implying non-relatedness to the world. For Hartshorne, God in the abstract nature, God's being, may in a way escape from the temporal flux, but a living natural God is related to the world of becoming, which entails a divine becoming as well if the world in some way is internally related to God. The classical theist's alternative to this view suggests that all realtionships to God are external to divinity, threatening not only God's love, but also God's nobility. A dog's being behind a particular rock affects the dog in certain ways, thus this relation is an internal relation to the dog. But it does not affect the rock, whose relationship with the dog is external to the rock's nature. Does this not show the superiority of canine consciousness, which is aware of the rock, to rocklike

existence, which is unaware of the dog?  Is it not
therefore peculiar that God has been described solely in
rocklike terms:  pure actuality, permanence, only having
external relations, unmoved, being not becoming?

It might be wondered at this point, as perhaps was
wondered by Thoreau, why classical theism has been so
popular among theists, since it has so many defects.
Hartshorne suggests at least four reasons:  (1) It is
simpler to accept one pole and reject the other of
contrasting (or better, correlative, non-invidious)
categories rather than to show how each, in its own
appropriate fashion, applies to an aspect of the divine
nature.  Yet the simplicity of calling God "the
absolute" can come back to haunt the classical theist if
absoluteness precludes relativity in the sense of
relatedness to the world.  (2) If the decision to accept
monopolarity has been made, it is simpler to identify
God as the absolute than to identify God as the most
relative.  Yet this does not deny divine relatedness,
nor that God, who loves all, would therefore have to be
related to all.  That is, God may well be the most
relative of all as well as the most absolute of all, in
the sense that, and to the extent that, both of these
are excellences.  God is absolute and relative in

different aspects of the divine nature. If this sounds inconsistent, consider that at each moment of his life Thoreau changed, if only by getting older, yet his identity as Henry David Thoreau remained permanent in the midst of all these changes. Cannot the same be said of God, only supremely so?

(3) There are emotional considerations favoring divine permanence, as found in the longing to escape the risks and uncertainties of life. But even if these considerations obtain, they should not blind us to other emotional considerations, like those which give us the solace that comes from knowing that the outcome of our sufferings and volitions makes a difference in the divine life, which, if it is all loving, would certainly not be unmoved by the sufferings of creatures. (4) It is seen as more easily made compatible with monotheism. But the innocent monotheistic contrast between the one and the many deals with God as an individual, not with the dogmatic claim that the divine individual itself cannot have parts or aspects of relatedness to the world.

In short, the divine being becomes, or better, the divine becoming is--God's being and becoming form a single reality:

> There is no law of logic against
> attributing contrasting predicates
> to the same individual, provided
> they apply to diverse aspects of
> this individual.[18]

The remedy for "ontolatry," the worship of being, is not
the contrary pole, "gignolatry," the worship of
becoming:

> God is neither being as contrasted
> to becoming nor becoming as
> contrasted to being; but
> categorically supreme becoming in
> which there is a factor of
> categorically supreme being, as
> contrasted to inferior becoming, in
> which there is inferior being.[19]

The divine becoming is more ultimate than the divine
being in process theism only for the reason that it is
more inclusive.

Hartshorne's theism, therefore, is: (1) dipolar
because excellences are found on both sides of the above
contrasting (that is, correlative, non-invidious)
categories; (2) a neoclassical theism because it relies
on the belief that the classical theist (especially St.

Anselm) was on the right track when he described God as the supremely excellent, all-worshipful, greatest conceivable being, except that the classical theist did an insufficient job of thinking through the logic of perfection; (3) a process theism in that it sees the need for God to become in order for God to be called perfect, but not at the expense of God's always (that is, permanently) being greater than all others; (4) a theism which can be called panentheism, which literally means "all in God." God is neither completely removed from the world, in other words unmoved by it, as in classical theism, nor completely identified with the world, as in pantheism. Rather, God is: (a) world-inclusive in the sense that God cares for all the world, and all feelings in the world--especially suffering feelings--are felt by God; and (b) transcendent in the sense that God is greater than any other being, especially because of God's unity, goodness, and love. Thus, Hartshorne rejects the conception of God as an unmoved mover not knowing the moving world (Aristotle); the unmoved mover inconsistently knowing and loving the moving world (classical theism); and the unmoved mover knowing an ultimately unmoving, or at least non-contingent, world (Stoics, Spinoza, pantheism).

Two final objections that may be raised by the
classical theist should be considered. To the rather
simple-minded objection that if God changed, God would
not be perfect, for if God were perfect there would be
no need to change, Hartshorne makes this rather obvious
reply (obvious, at least, to those who have thought
carefully about these matters): in order to be
supremely excellent God must at any particular time be
the greatest conceivable being, the all-worshipful
being. But at a later time, or in a new situation where
some creature that previously did not suffer now
suffers, God has new opportunities to exhibit divine
excellence. That is, God's perfection does not just
allow God to change, but requires God to change.[20]

The other objection might be that God is neither
one nor many, neither actual nor potential, etc.,
because no human concept whatsoever applies to God
literally or univocally, but at most analogically. The
classical theist or mystic or Thoreau scholar would say,
perhaps, that God is more unitary than unity, more
actual than actuality as humanly known. Yet one wonders
how the classical theist or mystic or Thoreau scholar,
once the insufficiency of human conceptions has been
admitted, can legitimately give a favored status to one

side (the left side) of conceptual contrasts at the
expense of the other. Why, Hartshorne asks, if God is
more simple than the one, is God not also more complex
in terms of relatedness to beings in nature than the
many? Analogical predication and negative theology can
just as easily fall victim to the monopolar prejudice as
can univocal predication. To be agent and patient is in
truth incomparably better than being either alone.

My thesis in this chapter is that Thoreau is a
dipolar theist. The evidence that Thoreau's God is a
God of becoming, a God to whom the predicates on the
right side are applicable, is massive:

> The good Hebrew Revelation takes no
> cognizance of all this cheerful
> snow. Is there no religion for the
> temperate and frigid zones? We
> know of no scripture which records
> the pure benignity of the gods on a
> New England winter night.[21]

Thoreau sees divinity in his Indian guide in the Maine
woods, Joe Polis; in some ways he sees even more
divinity in Joe Polis than in white men, signaling a
holiness in being close to nature.[22] The divine is also
disclosed in friendship.[23] God can be recognized both

in the poet[24] and in our senses, which are themselves a
high heaven.  Consider the following remarkable
quotation:

> May we not <u>see</u> God?  Are we to be
> put off and amused in this life, as
> it were with a mere allegory?  Is
> not Nature, rightly read, that of
> which she is commonly taken to be
> the symbol merely?[25]

Both human beings and other natural objects
exemplify Thoreau's immanent God, but it is the human
being-in-nature that is the most divine and most
startling of all natural facts.[26]:

> I cannot come nearer to God and
> Heaven/Than I live to Walden even.[27]

It should therefore be no surprise that for Thoreau the
destruction of the natural environment is a crime no
less than sacrilege[28]:

> My profession is to be always on the
> alert to find God in nature, to know
> his lurking places, to attend all
> the oratorios, the operas, in

nature....To watch for, describe,

all the divine features which I

detect in Nature.[29]

Divine becoming, for Thoreau, culminates in the present,
in anticipation of the future.[30] And this culmination
includes God's feelings for all of the images of God in
time, themselves partly divine, like the bream[31] or the
rainbow:

After the rain He sets his bow in

the heavens!....Is not the rainbow a

faint vision of God's face? How

glorious should be the life of man

passed under his arch![32]

The evidence for divine transcendence also is easy
to find, as when Thoreau compares the relationship
between a human being and an insect to that between God
and a human being.[33] God is not exactly the apotheosis
of wildness in the sense that God, in addition to being
found in the wilderness, is also ineffable, as was seen
in Chapter Two in the Lumen quotation. Or better, the
"Almighty is wild above all" (my emphasis).[34] As in
some types of Platonism, the most powerful metaphor for
divine transcendence is the sun, which Thoreau describes

as his private sun, seen by him alone at the top of a
long mountain climb. Alluding to the allegory of the
cave, Thoreau describes his descent as follows:

> I sank down again into that "forlorn
> world," from which the celestial sun
> had hid his visage....I....found
> myself in the region of cloud and
> drizzling rain, and the inhabitants
> affirmed that it had been a cloudy
> and drizzling day wholly.[35]

Wolf provides a fine list of names for God used by
Thoreau, and many of them illustrate attributes on the
left side of the above polar contrasts. Without a doubt
the influence of the Bible on Thoreau, much commented
on, prevents him from being a pantheist, even if he does
react against classical theism.[36] God at least
partially transcends time and space,[37] hence we can
understand exactly why Thoreau tells us about the skills
needed for us to approach God as transcendent:

> I hear beyond the range of sound,
> I see beyond the range of sight.[38]

Thoreau is certainly aware of the two poles in
God's nature and of how they are related. His theism is
not only dipolar like Hartshorne's, but is also

neoclassical in that Thoreau reshapes classical theism
so as to do more justice to the immanence of God.  Wolf,
however, alerts us to the fact that Thoreau never
initiated the word "pantheism" as a description of his
position.[39]  Although Thoreau had little interest in
clarifying his metaphysical stance, that does not mean
we cannot, or should not, do so.  His theism is dipolar,
neoclassical, includes process within god, and can also
perhaps be called a variety of panentheism.[40]  All
natural feelings--even nonhuman feelings--affect God,
but unlike in pantheism God is not exhausted by nature.
Rather than saying that God is in nature it is more
accurate to say that nature is in God.

   Some striking images of panentheism are developed
by Thoreau himself:

> By usurer's craft...we strive to
>
> retain and increase the divinity in
>
> us, when infinitely the greater part
>
> of divinity is out of us.[41]

Or again:

> If nature is our mother, is not God
>
> much more?[42]

Just as an individual is contained in its mother's womb,
so is the whole natural world contained in God.

> I will be thankful that I see so
> much as one side of a celestial
> idea, one side of the rainbow and
> the sunset sky, the face of God
> alone.[43]

Presumably the divine "head" lies beyond us in some way,
just as our own identities transcend our experiences at
any particular moment.  And just as the top of a
mountain can symbolize God as transcendent, we can
ascend all the while in awe, an ascent which implies
that the path itself is divine it that it is as inte-
grally connected to the mountain as the peak.  The world
is an integral whole, a cosmos, at the very least
because of God's ability to feel and care for all.  A
friend can "reflect a ray of God to me."[44]

All of this indicates that the world of becoming is
included in God's eternity (or as Hartshorne would put
it, in God's everlastingness), such that natural beings
can, if viewed in terms of their causal efficacy on an
everlasting God, be seen to bridge the gap between the
two poles of God's character.[45]  Thoreau's sister Sophia
once said that Bronson Alcott understood her brother's
religiosity best, and Alcott noticed that Thoreau showed
concern even for the fall of a sparrow because, it

seems, the sparrow in its own way contributes to the divine life.[46] But this gets us ahead of the story a bit, and into the major concern of Chapter Four. First we must consider how Thoreau's dipolar theism can be called Platonic.

It might be objected that my dipolar interpretation of Thoreau is highly unlikely because he never read Hartshorne. This charge may be a bit too hasty, however. Although the words were not used in antiquity, panentheism or dipolar theism are as old as Plato. One can easily be a dipolar theist in spite of oneself. From Chapter Two it should be obvious that Thoreau was self-consciously a follower of Plato. In short, if Plato were a dipolar theist or panentheist, it would not be an exotic guess to suspect that it was through him that Thoreau got his dipolar theism.

Certain Platonic texts are obvious sources. In the Sophist (246-249) the Eleatic Stranger develops the mature Platonic metaphysics, which is opposed by both the "giants," who are the materialists (or, we might say, the pantheists) who drag everything down from the heaven to earth; and the "gods," (or, we might say, the classical theists) who defend their position somewhere in the heights of the unseen. Reality is dyadic for

Plato, in that each instance of it contains both
internal and external relations, and is constituted by
anything (being or becoming) which has dynamis, the
power to affect or be affected by something else.[47]
Even in the Republic Plato avoids what many Platonists
have assumed to be the Platonic position: unbridled
worship of being. As we have seen, the task of the
philosopher (501B) is to glance frequently in two
directions. Thoreau had a yearning for the One
underlying the many, but also an appreciation of the
extent to which each of the many was itself possessive
of a certain degree of unity, or else each of these
would not be a tree, this cloud, et al.

Perhaps the most convincing studies of Plato's
theism and of the dyadic character of being in Plato,
have been done by Leonard Eslick, who relies on
Hartshorne, whom Eslick cites as the first to recognize
Plato as a dipolar theist.[48] There are two significant
ways in which Plato talks about God (theos). First, he
inherited from Parmenides the notion that being is
eternal, immutable, and self-same. This notion was the
starting point for the tradition of classical, monopolar
theism. "The extent to which Plato is committed to such
an absolute schism between being and becoming...would

seem to dictate for him a similar exclusion from divinity of all shadow of change."[49] This tendency is evidenced in Book Two and elsewhere in the Republic, the Phaedo (78-80), and the Symposium (202-203); and it is evidenced in some of Thoreau's writings cited above, including the Lumen quotation. However, as Eslick and others hold, there is no textual foundation for the popular identification of Plato's God with the transcendent Form of the Good, nor even with the world of Forms, either as a whole or in part.[50] Even when talking about divine eternity and immutability, the Platonic locus for divinity is psyche or nous. It comes as a shock to some readers of Plato who have read only the Republic, Phaedo, and Symposium that in the Phaedrus (245, etc.) Eros is claimed to be divine. Here Plato discovers, according to Eslick, a new, dynamic meaning for perfection, similar to the one Hartshorne defends and to the one exemplified by Thoreau when he talks about God as immanent.[51] The perfection that is dynamic is the perfection of life itself, treated not only in the Phaedrus but in Book Ten of the Laws as well.

In the Timaeus and the Sophist both poles in Plato's theism are brought together: the perfection of divine immutability and the perfection of divine life.

The former is identified in the Timaeus with the
Demiurge, who eternally and without change contemplates,
but is not identical with, the archetypal models, the
eternal Forms. The latter is identified with the
World-Soul--who is close to Thoreau's panpsychism, a
notion which is discussed in the notes and in Chapter
Four. The World-Soul's essence is self-motion, and is
depicted as posterior to the Demiurge.[52] The motions of
psychic life include both actions and passions. In
fact, in the Sophist, as has been noticed above, reality
is identified with dynamis or power, specifically the
power to affect or be affected by others. Aristotle
attests to the fact that reality (even divine reality),
for Plato, is the joint product of the One and the
Indefinite Dyad.[53] Unfortunately, Aristotle's own
notion of God loses the character of divine immanence,
of God as the Thoreauvian soul of the world. Even more
unfortunate is the fact that Plotinus and others who
became identified as followers of Plato were with
respect to their descriptions of God at times
Aristotelians.

It is not unreasonable to speculate that Thoreau
saw the inadequacies of latter day Platonists. In that
Wordsworth struggled his way to panentheism it is not

unlikely that Thoreau could have done the same, relying explicitly or implicitly on Plato.[54]  In any event, what several commentators have noticed in Thoreau's thought on God makes much more sense when Platonic-Hartshornian dipolar theism is kept in mind:  along with Wolf we can agree that the real issue in Thoreau's thought on God is whether God is immanent without remainder,[55] with Pickard we can concur that the religious quest of Walden was to "discover the spiritual laws which are a part of nature yet beyond it"[56] and with Bronson Alcott we can acknowledge that Thoreau's religiosity was both "animal and ideal."[57]

The mistake made by many interpreters of Thoreau should now be clear:  divine immanence is not necessarily incompatible with divine transcendence, and the eclectic nature of Thoreau's thought is not necessarily a sign of inconsistency on his part in that correlative concepts are not contradictory.  The reconciliation of correlative concepts may well be the Archimedes lever of criticism of Thoreau.  As we will see, reality is organic unity for him, but this reality can only be discursively revealed as two, like centripetal and centrifugal forces in equilibrium.[58] Plato's dipolar logic is thus not only a fruitful tool

that can be used in the analysis of Thoreau, but perhaps
an indispensable tool if one wants to avoid
deconstructionist anarchy.

NOTES: CHAPTER THREE

[1] Anderson, p. 172.

[2] Ibid., p. 173.

[3] Matthew 10: 28.

[4] Writings, 12, pp. 293-294.

[5] John B. Pickard, "The Religion of 'Higher Laws',"
in Richard Ruland, ed., Twentieth Century
Interpretations of Walden (Englewood Cliffs, New Jersey:
Prentice-Hall, 1968), p. 87.

[6] Ibid., p. 88.

[7] For Greeley's article in the New York Tribune of
June 13, 1849, see Walter Harding, ed., Thoreau: A
Century of Criticism (Dallas: Southern Methodist
University Press, 1965), pp. 3, 4, 7; for Krutch see
Henry David Thoreau (New York: Dell, 1965), p. 180.

[8] Willard Thorpe, "The Huckleberry Party," Thoreau
Society Bulletin (Summer, 1952).

[9] Wolf, p. 15, claims that Oriental thought may have
led Thoreau to something like pantheism just as
Wordsworth was led to pantheism; also, see pp. 151, 157,
165. See my article, "Wordsworth's Panentheism,"
forthcoming in The Wordsworth Circle, where I show that
Wordsworth was no more a pantheist than Thoreau.

[10] Anderson, pp. 65, 247.

[11] Cameron, Transcendental Apprenticeship, pp. 218-

220.

[12]Paul Elmer More, "A Hermit's Notes on Thoreau," in Walter Harding, ed., Thoreau: A Century of Criticism (Dallas: Southern Methodist University Press, 1965). From Atlantic Monthly (June, 1901).

[13]Writings, 7, p. 276.

[14]Ibid., 8, pp. 468-469. Also see Wolf, pp. 111-112.

[15]See Hartshorne's Man's Vision of God (New York: Harper and Brothers, 1941); The Divine Relativity (New Haven: Yale University Press, 1948); Reality as Social Process (Boston: Beacon Press, 1953); Philosophers Speak of God (Chicago: University of Chicago Press, 1953); A Natural Theology for Our Time (LaSalle, Illinois: Open Court, 1967); Creative Synthesis and Philosophic Method (LaSalle, Illinois: Open Court, 1970); Insights and Oversights of Great Thinkers (Albany: State University of New York Press, 1983); Omnipotence and Other Theological Mistakes (Albany: State University of New York Press, 1984). In a chapter on Thoreau and Emerson, Hartshorne denies that Emerson is a panentheist and implies he is a pantheist. The fact that Hartshorne does not say the same about Thoreau is noteworthy. See Creativity in American Philosophy

(Albany:  State University of New York Press, 1984), p.
49.  On pp. 281-282 Hartshorne indicates that William
Ellery Channing was working his way toward dipolar
theism.  This shows the plausibility of my claims
regarding Thoreau.

[16]See Hartshorne's The Logic of Perfection
(LaSalle, Illinois:  Open Court, 1962) and Anselm's
Discovery (LaSalle, Illinois: Open Court, 1965).  Also
see J. Prescott Johnson, "The Ontological Argument in
Plato."

[17]Hartshorne, Philosophers Speak of God, p. 3.

[18]Ibid., pp. 14-15.

[19]Ibid., p. 24

[20]For Hartshorne, God must be as great as possible
at any particuar time or else God would not be the
greatest conceivable being.  But new moments bring with
them new possibilities for greatness, possibilities
which God must realize in the best way possible if God
is the greatest, or better, the unsurpassable.  This
means that God is greater than a being that is not God,
but God can always, must always, surpass previous
greatness in the divine nature.  This does not mean that
God's earlier existence was inferior, because it was at
that particular time the greatest conceivable existence.

[21] Henry D. Thoreau, _Excursions_ (Boston:  Houghton Mifflin, 1883), pp. 133-134.

[22] Harding and Bode, _Correspondence_, p. 491.

[23] Wolf, p. 72.

[24] _A Week_, p. 340.

[25] Ibid., p. 382.

[26] _Writings_, 8, p. 208.

[27] _Walden_, p. 193.

[28] Wolf, p. 106.

[29] _Writings_, 8, p. 472.

[30] _Walden_, p. 97.  Wolf, p. 121, interprets this as the (classical theistic) "eternal now," but the fact that Thoreau says God_culminates in the present indicates a divine _passage_ from the past to the present. Wolf is correct, however, but for the wrong reason, that Thoreau's position is Platonic here.  Thoreau assures us that although the future may add something to the divine nature, God will no more _be_ God than God is right now.

[31] _Writings_, 17, p. 359.

[32] Ibid., 10, 128.

[33] _Walden_, p. 332.  Also see Wolf, p. 105.

[34] Wolf, pp. 107, 122, 185.  Also see _Writings_, 10, p. 482.

[35] _A Week_, p. 190.

[36]See Wolf, pp. 158, 162, 165.

[37]Writings, 8, pp. 214-215, 497.  Also see Walden, p. 332, where Thoreau refers to God as the great "Benefactor and Intelligence."

[38]From "Inspiration."  See Carl Bode, ed., Collected Poems of Henry David Thoreau (Baltimore: Johns Hopkins, 1965), pp. 231-232.  Also see Chapter Two, note 82, above.

[39]Wolf, p. 156, points out that when the label "pantheist" was applied to Thoreau he replied:  "if that be the name of me" (my emphasis).  See Harding and Bode, eds., Correspondence, p. 294.

[40]Only in Wolf's excellent study, as far as I know, can there be found a treatment of Thoreau's thoughts on God from the perspective of process philosophy or panentheism.  See pp. 157, 172-174, where Wolf uses Alfred North Whitehead (Hartshorne's great teacher), Teilhard de Chardin, and Hartshorne.

[41]Writings, 7, p. 386.

[42]Ibid., 7, p. 326.

[43]Ibid., 9, p. 174.  To use another metaphor, the universe is a society of which one member (God) is preeminent, just as human beings are societies of which the mental part is preeminent.  That is, we are cells in

the divine organism. Also see Cavell, p. 137.

[44]A Week, p. 285.

[45]Writings, 14, pp. 222-223.

[46]See Thoreau Society Bulletin 78 (Winter, 1962).

[47]See my Plato's Philosophy of History on the Sophist; and see "Rorty on Plato as an Edifier," Philosophia (Athens) 13-14 (1983-1984): 142-153.

[48]Leonard Eslick, "Plato as Dipolar Theist," Process Studies 12 (1982), pp. 243-251. Also his "The Dyadic Character of Being in Plato," Modern Schoolman 21 (1953-1954), pp. 11-18.

[49]Eslick, "Plato as Dipolar Theist," p. 244.

[50]Paul Elmer More's work on Plato, alluded to earlier in this chapter, is The Religion of Plato (Princeton: Princeton University Press, 1921). The position which identifies the Form of the Good with God relies on the neoplatonic interpretation of Plato popular in late antiquity, an interpretation which greatly influenced Thomas Taylor and, to a lesser degree, Thoreau. Also see Wolf, p. 174.

[51]Eslick, "Plato as Dipolar Theist," p. 245.

[52]See Timaeus (34B), where it is quite clear that the World-Soul is a blessed God and (30-31), where the World-Soul is described as perfect; in the Philebus (30)

the World-Soul is fairest and most precious; also see the Laws (896-899). It should be mentioned that although the World-Soul is posterior to the Demiurge, Plato's temporalizing of creation in the Timaeus is admittedly mythic. It is possible that Plato's World-Soul is more inclusive than the Demiurge, making Plato's dipolar theism closer to Hartshornian panentheism than some suppose. Finally, Thoreau's comparison of "the vitals of the globe" with "the vitals of the animal body" is much like Plato's depiction of the earth as the divine animal. Thoreau is quite frank in saying: "There is nothing inorganic," and that the earth itself is living poetry. See Chapter Four, as well as Walden, pp. 306, 308-309.

[53]Metaphysics A.

[54]See Anderson, pp. 96, 225, where it is claimed that "Tintern Abbey" taught Thoreau a "wise passivity" before nature, that when "The Prelude" was made available in 1850 Thoreau immediately bought a copy, and that Thoreau often alludes to "Intimations of Immortality" in his Journal. I would like to note that one of the first great dipolar theists in the modern world was Socinus; see Hartshorne's Philosophers Speak of God. As is well known, Socinus in many ways provided

the intellectual foundation for Unitarianism, which,
through Emerson and other sources, was no doubt
influential in the development of Thoreau's attitudes
toward God and religion.  Thus, Socinian ideas, as
transmitted through the Unitarian tradition, provide
another indirect (as in Wordsworth's case) source for
Thoreau's Platonism and dipolar theism.

[55]Wolf, p. 158.

[56]Pickard, p. 90.

[57]See Odell Shepard, ed., The Journals of Bronson
Alcott (Boston:  Little, Brown, 1938), pp. 318-350.

[58]See Richard Harter Fogle, The Idea of Coleridge's
Criticism (Berkeley:  University of California Press,
1962), p. 4, for similarity between Thoreau and
Coleridge regarding dipolarity.

# CHAPTER FOUR: THOREAU, SAINTHOOD, AND VEGETARIANISM

Anderson[1] speaks for most scholars when he says that Thoreau's vegetarianism has proved a stumbling block for readers. His diet in _Walden_,[2] according to Anderson, strikes the modern critic as the aberrant dream of a food crank, leading Anderson to defend Thoreau only by saying that his treatment of food in _Walden_ is symbolic or metaphoric,[3] presumably because Thoreau's vegetarian beliefs cannot be taken seriously or literally. Anderson maintains in his _apologia_ that although Thoreau advocated vegetarianism, at least he was not a "fanatic."[4] Seybold's defense of Thoreau is equally unenthusiastic. Despite his vegetarianism Thoreau had no "foolish scruples."[5] Joseph Jones compares nineteenth century vegetarianism with phrenology and mesmerism,[6] and concludes that most of us probably think that Thoreau was a food crank who was fair game for fads. "The diet reformers," writes Jones, "managed for a time to sell many earnest seekers a bill of groceries."[7] Jones treats this bill of groceries with about as much respect as he would a bottle of snake oil.

One of the few commentators who treats Thoreau's advocacy of vegetarianism favorably is one of his first biographers, Henry Salt, who was a vegetarian himself.

Salt says: "Humanity to animals was one of the most conspicuous virtues in Thoreau's character, and is constantly, if indirectly, advocated in his writings."[8] Salt says little else about Thoreau's vegetarianism; his silence is regrettable in that his own book on the topic is well argued.[9] He surely <u>could</u> have said much more about Thoreau's position, but for some reason did not. In this chapter I will take up Thoreau and Salt's cause and state what will probably be an unpopular thesis: (1) Thoreau's vegetarian position makes sense and can be given a rational defense today; and (2) Thoreau's approach to vegetarianism exemplifies a type of sainthood or moral excellence that forces all moral agents to at least consider the possibility that meat-eating is morally reprehensible. No doubt the reader of this chapter will assume I have bitten off more than I can chew, but I promise to swallow whatever embarrassment I bring to myself because of the position I take. My tone will be both analytic--in that I will be examining Thoreau's texts and showing how Thoreau got his thoughts on vegetarianism from Plato, as Bronson Alcott noticed[10]--and exhortative in that I will be suggesting that Thoreau was right about vegetarianism. (I will deal in Chapter Five with the controversial issue as to whether textual analysis should, or even can, have the moral import I assume here.) My first task will be to offer an analysis of the term "sainthood," an analysis which will take me to the heart of the issue at hand.

The best conceptual framework I know of that deals with the notion of sainthood or heroism is J.O. Urmson's seminal philosophical article "Saints and Heroes."[11] I will use these roughly synonymous words in a purely moral sense with no religious implications regarding miracles or the like. Urmson notes that:

> Moral philosophers tend to
> discriminate, explicitly or
> implicitly, three types of action
> from the point of view of moral
> worth. First, they recognize
> actions that are a duty, or
> obligatory, or that we ought to
> perform, treating these terms as
> approximately synonymous; second,
> they recognize actions that are
> right in so far as they are
> permissible from a moral standpoint
> and not ruled out by moral
> considerations, but that are not

morally required of us...; third,
they recognize actions that are
wrong, that we ought not to do.[12]
Urmson rightly holds that this threefold classification
is inadequate because it leaves out of consideration a
certain class of actions performed in a heroic or
saintly way. But not all heroic or saintly actions are
outside this classification, as the following analysis
of "saint" indicates:

A person may be called a saint (1)
if he does his duty regularly in
contexts in which inclination,
desire, or self-interest would lead
most people not to do it, and does
so as a result of abnormal self-
control...(2) if he does his duty in
contexts in which inclination or
self-interest would lead most men
not to do it, not...by abnormal
self-control, but without effort...
(3) if he does actions that are far
beyond the limits of his duty.[13]

That is, saint$_1$ and saint$_2$ achieve their heroic status by merely meeting their duties when others fail, and saint$_3$ achieves sainthood by going "above and beyond the call of duty." The actions of saint$_3$ are usually called supererogatory (<u>erogatio</u> is Latin for payment).[14]

A preliminary example of a saintly action that is <u>not</u> supererogatory would be the case of a doctor who stayed by his patients in a plague-ridden city when all of his fellow doctors fled, and supererogation can be seen in the case of a doctor who <u>volunteered</u> to go to a plague-ridden city. If the first doctor were interviewed after the plague he might well say, "I only did my (Hippocratic) duty." But only a modesty so excessive as to appear false could make the second doctor say the same.[15] Or again, a government official who swears never to give information to the enemy, and remains silent even after torture by the enemy, is a non-supererogatory hero, but Fr. Kolbe, the Franciscan priest who <u>asked</u> the Nazis to kill him, instead of a man with a family who was supposed to be killed, is a hero$_3$.

Although the actions of saint$_3$ are saintly par excellence, we should not forget how hard the way of duty may be, and that doing one's duty can at times deserve to be called heroic or saintly. J.S. Mill puts

116

the matter a bit too commercially when he says that a duty can be exacted from persons as a debt since it is a minimum requirement for living together.[16] Yet Mill's intent is well taken by Urmson:

> ...while life in a world without its
> saints and heroes would be
> impoverished, it would only be poor
> and not necessarily brutish or short
> as when basic duties are neglected.
> If we are to exact basic duties like
> debts, and censure failures, such
> duties must be, in ordinary
> circumstances, within the capacity
> of the ordinary man.[17]

To take a parallel from law, Prohibition asked too much of the American people, and as citizens got used to breaking the law, a lowering of respect for the law followed.[18] Likewise, if we expect supererogation from moral agents, we might not only be disappointed, but we might also notice a general disregard for duties as well:

> A line must be drawn between what we
> can expect and demand from others
> and what we can merely hope for and
> receive with gratitude when we get
> it.[19]

With these categories as a background, what can be said about Thoreau's vegetarianism? It is certainly not a practice to be prohibited, which means that it is either permissible, or a duty, or supererogatory. To say that Thoreau's position is merely permissible is uninformative, and seems to ignore the noble aspirations that Thoreau has in "Higher Laws," the chapter in Walden where he develops his thought on this topic. And as Pickard emphasizes, "Higher Laws" contains the "quintessence of Thoreau's religious insights."[20] That is, here Thoreau attempts to "transform the brutish and unclean into direct channels of grace for sainthood" (my emphasis). Unfortunately, by emphasizing Thoreau's "ascetic discipline"[21] rather than his very Greek moderation (sophrosyne), Pickard might unwittingly lead us to assume that Thoreau's "Higher Laws" are supererogatory. But it remains to be decided whether Thoreau's vegetarianism is a duty or supererogatory. One might suspect that Thoreau's status would be more exalted if his vegetarianism were supererogatory. If his vegetarianism is "above and beyond" duty, however, his conduct does not necessarily have implications for we who are mere mortals, which makes reading Thoreau a bit too tame for my taste. What can be stated with assurance at this point is that the "Higher Laws" are central for an understanding of Thoreau's thought.[22]

If one _assumes_ that there is no duty to abstain from animal flesh, then Thoreau's vegetarianism would appear to be supererogatory. Since most commentators make this assumption, it is not surprising that they see him going beyond the call of duty in his dietary regimen. Emerson is illustrative here when he quotes Aristotle in reference to Thoreau:

> One who surpasses his fellow
> citizens in virtue is no longer a
> part of the city. Their law is not
> for him, since he is a law to
> himself.[23]

To use Emerson's terms, "their" law comprises the realm of duty, whereas Thoreau's "law" is above duty. But Emerson's apparent praise of Thoreau here is hardly praise at all. Since we are not required to go beyond

duty, Thoreau's "law" becomes largely irrelevant.
Perhaps this is why Emerson can so easily criticize
Thoreau by saying:

> ...instead of engineering for all
> America, he was the captain of a
> huckleberry party. Pounding beans
> is good to the end of pounding
> empires one of these days; but if,
> at the end of years, it is still
> beans![24]

Anderson and Jones[25] also see Thoreau's
vegetarianism as supererogatory. The former notices
Thoreau's tendency to divide the word "extravagant" into
Latin components:  going beyond. And the latter sees
Thoreau's vegetarianism as part of his campaign of
simplification:

> The terms of the Walden sojourn were
> deliberately experimental and of
> limited duration.

That is, eventually Thoreau would come back home and eat
better foods.

Is it obvious that Thoreau's vegetarianism is
supererogatory? Might it be the case that "higher laws"
are indeed moral <u>laws</u> that as moral agents we have a

duty to obey? That these laws are higher does not necessarily imply supererogation, but might only mean that they are higher than the normal (meat-eating) allegiances of most human beings, which are perhaps less rigorous than they should be. If I am right in these suspicions, then Thoreau can legitimately be called a saint$_1$ with respect to his eating, a hero who merely met his duty by struggling against the habits of his meat-eating fellows. I will offer two arguments to establish vegetarianism as a duty, to be followed by an analysis of the relevant texts in Walden and elsewhere.

Thoreau advocated vegetarianism for various reasons. The practice seems to have been a part of his ascetical desire to purify the soul as a preparation for contemplative life.[26] It also seems to have been more conducive to his imagination.[27] Practically speaking, Thoreau found eating meat unclean, especially because he did his own butchering.[28] These reasons are either vague or they are not compelling. What has not been noticed are the most sophisticated reasons for vegetarianism that are evidenced in Walden: the arguments from sentiency and marginal cases. Thoreau obviously does not present these arguments as philosophical proofs; that was not his style. But his

position presupposes an understanding of philosophical
arguments for vegetarianism.  As I argued in Chapter
One, it can be held that:

> ...the style of Walden can be
> deceptively simple, in the American
> tradition (inaugurated by Franklin)
> of the natural as opposed to the
> bookish writer.  But the experienced
> reader learns to see through this
> homespun disguise to the body of
> learning buried beneath.[29]

The learning Thoreau digested regarding vegetarianism
came from many sources. His familiarity with Oriental
vegetarianism shows in the text.[30]  And the influence of
Wiliam A. Alcott and other transcendental vegetarians
has been ably treated by Jones.[31]

The most important influences on Thoreau's thoughts
on vegetarianism, however, were Porphyry and Iamblichus,
two ancient Greek neoplatonic vegetarians that Thoreau
read.  It is no accident, as we will see, that these
figures were self-professed Platonists.  Anderson[32]
highlights the passages from Thoreau's commonplace book
which prove that he read both Porphyry's On Abstinence
from Animal Food and Iamblichus's Life of Pythagoras.[33]

But Seybold holds[34] that although Thoreau and Porphyry reached the same conclusion, Thoreau's vegetarianism was not built on philosophical reasons. She says:

> Thoreau objected to animal food on
> the grounds that it was distasteful
> to prepare, that killing animals was
> a callous infliction of pain, and
> that it was better for an intel-
> lectual not to eat much of any food
> (my emphasis).

As I will show, objection to the callous infliction of pain is a philosophical reason against meat-eating.

Like Thoreau, Porphyry struggled with Christianity and rediscovered Pythagoras and Plato. Anderson is exactly right in claiming that the key to "Higher Laws" is understanding Porphyry's On Abstinence. Porphyry's pupil, Iamblichus, in a description of Pythagoras, may just as easily have described Thoreau: he advocated the study of nature as a way of life, he was particularly identified with Apollo, and he believed that animals deserve justice.[35] In fact, Pythagoras's vegetarian regimen is similar in many ways to the regimen in Walden (even in their common dislike of beans). Thoreau puns on the coenobitae, the Pythagorean comunes, when he

refers to the local commune of fishermen:    see no bites.
It must be granted that Thoreau read largely for
confirmation of his own beliefs, but what he read often
amplified these beliefs and carried them into the
precise form in which we find them in his texts.    Such
is the case regarding vegetarianism.

In Porphyry's book there are two arguments for
vegetarianism which, when used as heuristic guides,
enable us to get to the heart of Thoreau's beliefs in a
way that might not otherwise be posible.    I will present
in formal outline, very crudely in the language used by
philosophical vegetarians today, what Thoreau
exemplifies in the informal mode of the literary artist.
The argument from sentiency goes something like this:

1.  Any being that can suffer at the very
    least ought not to be forced to suffer
    unnecessarily.

2.  It is not necessary that we inflict
    suffering on animals so that we can eat,
    since eating vegetables can be very good
    for one's health.

3.  Therefore, to inflict unnecessary
    suffering on an animal so as to eat it is
    morally reprehensible or cruel.

As Jeremy Bentham put it, "The question is not, Can they
reason? nor Can they talk? but Can they _suffer_?"[36]
Animals raised for the table can suffer; plants, for all
we can tell, cannot. Some might suspect that an escape
from this argument can be found in "sneaking up" on the
animal to kill it painlessly. There are many ways to
respond to this objection (it does seem peculiar that
some think that pain is a "hurt" but killing is not),
one of which is through the argument from marginal
cases. Peter Singer puts it this way:

> The catch is that any such
> characteristic that is posessed by
> _all_ human beings will not be
> possessed _only_ by human beings. For
> example all humans, but not only
> humans, are capable of feeling pain;
> and while only humans are capable of
> solving complex mathematical
> problems, not all humans can do
> this. So it turns out that in the
> only sense in which we can truly
> say, as an assertion of fact, that
> all humans are equal, at least some

        members of other species are also
        "equal"--equal that is, to some
        humans.[37]

Theological statements of a human being's privileged
status cannot be philosophically justified.  Moreover to
say that we can legitimately eat animals because human
beings are rational, or autonomous, or just, or
language-users, etc., is not true of many human beings.
These "marginal cases" include infants, the mentally
enfeebled, and the like.  If we "lower" our standard to
that of sentiency (for example, the ability to
experience pain) so as to protect these people,[38] we
must also protect many animals, including those we eat.

    Or, as Tom Regan puts it,[39] if an animal has
characteristics a, b, c...z but lacks autonomy (or
reason or language) and a human being has
characteristics a, b, c...z but lacks autonomy (or
reason or language), then we have as much reason to
believe that the animal deserves respect as the human.
This respect would include not to be forced to suffer or
be killed unnecessarily.  The following text from
Porphyry deals with the argument from marginal cases,
and gives an indication of the sophistication of the
Greek vegetarianism with which Thoreau was familiar:

To compare plants, however, with
animals, is doing violence to the
order of things. For the latter are
naturally sensitive (aisthanesthai),
and, adapted to feel pain, to be
terrified and hurt (kai algein kai
phobeisthai kai blaptesthai); on
which account also they may be
injured (adikeisthai). But the
former are entirely destitute of
sensation, and in consequence of
this, nothing foreign, or evil
(kakon), or hurtful (blabe), or
injurious (adikia), can befall them.
For sensation is the principle of
all alliance (Kai gar oikeioseos
pases kai allotrioseos arche to
aisthanesthai)....And is it not
absurd (alogon), since we see that
many of our own species (anthropon)
live from sense alone (aisthesei
monon), but do not possess intellect
(noun) and reason (logon)...that no
justice is shown from us to the ox

that ploughs, the dog that is fed
with us, and the animals that
nourish us with their milk, and
adorn our bodies with their wool?
Is not such an opinion most
irrational and absurd?[40]

Now to Thoreau's own words. He certainly shows
evidence of agreement with the first premise of the
argument from sentiency. His position is quite clear:

No human being, past the thoughtless
age of boyhood, will wantonly murder
any creature, which holds its life
by the same tenure that he does.
The hare in its extremity cries like
a child. I warn you, mothers, that
my sympathies do not always make the
usual phil-anthropic distinctions.[41]

Thoreau holds that the hare suffers, and to kill it is
wanton murder; that the murder is wanton perhaps
signifies that it is unnecessary killing that Thoreau
finds objectionable. His philia (love) extends far
beyond, but not excluding, anthropos (humanity) to all
sentient life. Fish are also sentient, as can be seen
when the fisherman hooks a catch on his line:

> ...feeling a slight vibration along
> it, indicative of some life prowling
> about its extremity, of dull
> uncertain blundering purpose there,
> and slow to make up its mind.[42]

Although the purposes of animals are dull and uncertain, and although their minds are slow, the fact that they have purposes and minds at all is what Thoreau considers important. Thoreau is also clear about the second premise:

> A little bread or a few potatoes
> would have done as well.[43]

As well, presumably, as meat for a healthy diet. Consider the passage early on in Walden:

> One farmer says to me, "You cannot
> live on vegetable food solely for it
> furnishes nothing to make bones
> with;" and so he religiously devotes
> a part of his day to supplying his
> system with the raw material of
> bones; walking all the while he
> talks behind his oxen, which, with
> vegetable-made bones, jerk him and
> his lumbering plough along in spite

of every obstacle.  Some things are
really necessaries of life in some
circles, the most helpless and
diseased, which in others are
luxuries merely, and in others still
are entirely unknown.[44]

Thoreau sees that culturally determined "needs" are
different from biological ones.  As regards the latter,
food is necessary, but not animal food.[45]  In our
culture we have come to think that it would be terribly
difficult to abstain from meat but:

I learned from my two years'
experience that it would cost
incredibly little trouble to obtain
one's necessary food.[46]

In that Thoreau accepts the two premises of the
argument from sentiency, it is not surprising that he
also accepts the conclusion.  Thoreau came to
vegetarianism as an adult, and had to struggle against
the acceptance of meat-eating tradition that he was
exposed to as a gun-carrying child:

I did not pity the fishes nor the
worms.  This was habit.[47]

However:

> I have found repeatedly, of late
> years, that I cannot fish without
> falling a little in self-respect. I
> have tried it again and again. I
> have skill at it, and, like many of
> my fellows, a certain instinct for
> it, which revives from time to time,
> but always when I have done I feel
> that it would have been better if I
> had not fished...with every year I
> am less a fisherman, though without
> more humanity or even wisdom.[48]

Thoreau reached this same position regarding land
animals some time before.[49] Remembering Urmson we can
say that Thoreau was the sort of saint who only met his
duty ("without more humanity or even wisdom"); what
makes him saintly is his struggle to meet his duty when
others failed:

> Is it not a reproach that man is a
> carnivorous animal? True, he can
> and does live, in a great measure,
> by preying on other animals; but
> this is a miserable way,--as any one
> who will go to snaring rabbits, or

slaughtering lambs, may learn,--and
he will be regarded as a benefactor
of his race who shall teach man to
confine himself to a more innocent
and wholesome diet. Whatever my own
practice may be, I have no doubt
that it is a part of the destiny of
the human race, in its gradual
improvement, to leave off eating
animals, as surely as the savage
tribes have left off eating each
other when they came into contact
with the more civilized. If one
listens to the faintest but constant
suggestions of his genius, which are
certainly true, he sees not to what
extremes, or even insanity, it may
lead him; and yet that way as he
grows more resolute and faithful,
his road lies. The faintest assured
objection which one healthy man
feels will at length prevail over
the arguments and customs of
mankind.[50]

Like many of the great saints, Thoreau was tempted and,
on occasion, "sinned." But gradually he met his duty
with greater and greater ease, leading one to wonder
whether he ended up a $saint_2$ (see diagram 1). Whether
or not Thoreau was a $saint_1$ or a $saint_2$, however, is not
as important as the fact that he was <u>not</u> a $saint_3$ with
respect to his vegetarianism. His "conformity to higher
principles"[51] is only higher when compared to his former
(and mankind's present) wildness.[52] Thoreau appeals to
all of us, not just to those angelic disembodied <u>cogitos</u>
found in hagiography:

> <u>Our</u> whole life is startlingly moral.
> There is never an instant's truce
> between virtue and vice. Goodness
> is the only investment that never
> fails (my emphasis).[53]

Virtue forces us to consider what Thoreau finds
appealing in Mencius:

> That in which men differ from brute
> beasts is a thing very
> inconsiderable; the common herd lose
> it very soon; superior men preserve
> it carefully.[54]

In a way, we are all called to be "superior" to the
violation of duty; there is nothing impossible in our
becoming philosophers, if what is meant by a philosopher
is one who tries to:

> ...solve some of the problems of
> life, not only theoretically, but
> practically.[55]

That Thoreau was also persuaded by the argument from
marginal cases is not as obvious, but is suggested when
he says that no humane being will "murder _any_ creature"
(my emphasis), not even those creatures who value their
lives without the ability to reason.[56] Further, just as
culture has shaken off the practice of anthropophagy,
eventually it will have to develop an "innocent" diet
with respect to animals.[57] One can only infer from this
that eating non-human animals and eating human beings
are both "guilty" practices, albeit to different
degrees.

The major problem facing Thoreau's position is the
suggestion that if we take his principles seriously we
will have nothing left to eat, or at least nothing to
eat that we will not feel guilty about. It might be
alleged that Singer's criticism of St. Francis of Assisi
applies to Thoreau as well:

DIAGRAM 1

| TYPES OF MORAL ACTIONS | TYPES OF HEROISM-SAINTHOOD | THOREAU'S SAINTHOOD |
|---|---|---|
| A. Prohibited Acts | | |
| B. Permissible Acts | | |
| C. Duties | 1. Performs duty with great effort when others fail. | 1. Eats a vegetarian diet, but with difficulty at times. |
| | 2. Performs duty without effort when others fail. | 2. "...with every year I am less a fisherman...at present I am no fisherman at all ....I have no doubt that it is a part of the destiny of the human race, in its gradual |

DIAGRAM 1 CON'T

leave off eating
animals, as surely
as the savage
tribes have left
off eating each
other."

D. Supererogatory
Acts

3. Goes beyond duty.

> While this kind of ecstatic
> universal love can be a wonderful
> fountain of compassion and goodness,
> the lack of rational reflection can
> also do much to counteract its
> beneficial consequences. If we love
> rocks, trees, plants, larks, and
> oxen equally, we may lose sight of
> the essential differences between
> them, most importantly, the
> differences in degree of sentience.[58]

Thoreau comes dangerously close to this Franciscan
predicament when he says:

> The earth is all alive and covered
> with papillae. The largest pond is
> as sensitive to atmospheric changes
> as the globule of mercury in its
> tube.[59]

This might seem to be loose speech, but a deeper
analysis of the text reveals that the aliveness and
sensitivity of the earth that Thoreau speaks of are not
to be confused with sentiency per se, that is, the
ability to experience pleasure and pain in an intense
way. Wolf is correct in saying that there is nothing

inorganic for Thoreau, and that organic "stuff" is a means of communication with God,[60] but what do these statements mean?  That the earth is alive with a Bergsonian élan vital, and that nature must be viewed in a way "associated with human affections"[61] are not intuitively obvious propositions.

Plato and Hartshorne can again point the way. Three sorts of sentiency (S) can be distinguished, all three of which can be found in Plato, Thoreau, and Hartshorne in various ways under different labels.  S1 is sentiency at the microscopic level of cells, atomic particles, and the like, where contemporary physics has vindicated the positions of Plato and Thoreau.  The nightmare of determinism has faded, as reality in its fundamental constituents itself seems to have at least a partially indeterminate character of self-motion.  That is, the sum total of efficient causes from the past does not supply the sufficient cause to explain the behavior of the smallest units of becoming in the world.  Thoreau was wiser than he knew; little did he know that in twentieth century physics universal mechanism would give way to a cosmic dance.  S2 is sentiency per se, sentiency in the sense of feeling of feeling, found in animals and human beings, whereby beings with central

nervous systems or something like them can feel as
wholes, just as their consituent parts show
prefigurments of feeling on a local level. And feeling
_is_ localized; think of a knife stuck in the gut of any
vertebrate, or of sexual pleasure. S2 consists in
taking these local feelings and collecting them so that
an individual as a whole can feel what happens to its
parts, even if the individual partially transcends the
parts. Hurt my cells and you hurt _me_. S3 is divine
sentiency. If I am not mistaken, Thoreau shares with
Plato and Hartshorne the following four-term analogy:

$$S1 : S2 :: S2 : S3$$

As before, the universe is a society or an organism (a
Platonic World-Soul) of which one member (God, or the
Platonic Demiurge) is preeminent, just as human beings
are societies of cells of which the mental part is
preeminent. As was seen in Chapter Three, Thoreau is
happy to see God's face, if not the whole head of the
divine.

Neither Plato nor Thoreau nor Hartshorne could find
the following four-term analogy an adequate tool in
describing the cosmos:

$$S1 : \text{a table} :: S2 : \text{the "uni"verse}$$
$$\text{as a concatention of parts}$$

Or as Erazim Kohák puts it:

> Shall we conceive of the world
>
> around us and of ourselves in it as
>
> personal, a meaningful whole,
>
> honoring its order as continuous
>
> with the moral law of our own being
>
> and its beings as continuous with
>
> ours, bearing its goodness--or shall
>
> we conceive of it and treat it,
>
> together with ourselves, as
>
> impersonal, a chance aggregate of
>
> matter propelled by a blind force
>
> and exhibiting at most the
>
> ontologically random lawlike regu-
>
> larities of a causal order?

Mere matter on this Platonic, Thoreauvian, Kohákian,
Hartshornian view only appears when composites are taken
for singulars. For example, although tables or rocks do
not feel, there is feeling, however primitive, in them.
Plants are in a grey area between rocks and animals in
this regard. In that they are alive they are like
animals, but without central nervous systems they seem
to lack S2, even if their cells exhibit S1.

Although the eating of any food is to be denigrated
if done gluttonously, Thoreau makes it clear that:

> The fruits eaten temperately need
> not make us ashamed of our
> appetites, nor interrupt the
> worthiest pursuits.[62]

The same cannot be said of meats. If the meaning of
"fruits" is taken widely, Thoreau's point becomes
apparent: it is by no means <u>obvious</u> that plants
experience pain or have S2, hence they can legitimately
be eaten; animals, at least the ones raised for the
table or hunted or fished, obviously do have S2 and
ought not to be forced to suffer unnecessarily or be
deprived of a pleasurable life unnecessarily. Thoreau
has a certain sort of reverence for trees, but only more
primitive religious beliefs, like those of the Romans,
would allow one to see trees animated with souls worthy
of respect.[63] Despite Adams' contention that Thoreau
believed in transmigration, whereby a tree could be
inhabited by the soul of a dead human being,[64] Thoreau
felled trees and picked beans with equanimity. Contrast
this with his less than sanguine mood when he thought
about killing animals.

Thoreau was not unaware of another objection, which would claim that nature is a jungle where:

> The perch swallows the grubworm, the
> pickerel swallows the perch, and the
> fisherman swallows the pickerel; and
> so all the chinks of the scale of
> being are filled.[65]

But the men Thoreau refers to here, who have "some right to fish," are "wild men" who "never consulted with books." I am tempted to say, remembering Thoreau's confidence in the progress of human eating habits, that these men are in the childhood of the human race. Thoreau's displeasure is not so much directed at those primitive woodsmen who eat meat after courageously killing and butchering animals themselves, but at more "civilized" types who assume meat was created _ex nihilo_ by the grocer. This is only a veneer of "civilization" that is surpassed by a bloodless diet. Even after Thoreau's "conversion" to vegetarianism he had moments when "no morsel could have been too savage." "I could sometimes eat a friend rat with a good relish, _if it were necessary_" (my emphasis).[66] It may also be the case that Thoreau mentions the rat so as to push his reader into direct contact with repulsion to animal

food. The rat will eat virtually anything; will human
beings do the same? A related example showing Thoreau's
saintly attitude toward woodsmen can be seen when
Thoreau went to the Maine woods:

> Though I had not come a-hunting, and
> felt some compunctions about
> accompanying the hunters, I wished
> to see a moose near at hand....I
> went as reporter or <u>chaplain</u> to the
> hunters (my emphasis).[67]

Although a genetic approach (which pays careful
attention to the stages in Thoreau's career) to
Thoreau's vegetarianism is in some ways attractive, and
receives support from Thoreau's own admission that with
each year he moved further and further away from eating
animals, we should not fail to notice elements of
lifelong continuity in his stance. As early as 1837 he
asks:

> First, what is moral excellence?
> Not, surely, the mere
> acknowledgement of the divine origin
> of the Scriptures, and obedience to
> their dictates as such; nor yet an
> implicit compliance with the

requisitions of what may be termed
popular morality. It consists
rather in allowing the <u>religious</u>
sentiment to exercise a <u>natural</u> and
proper influence over our lives and
conduct--in acting from a sense of
<u>duty</u>, or, as we say, from principle.
The morally excellent, then, are
constantly striving to discover and
pursue the right. This is their
whole <u>duty</u>; for, in the inquiry
(regarding) what is right, <u>reason</u>
<u>alone</u> can decide, and her dictates
are ever identical with the dictates
of <u>duty</u>....The morally right ....As
it is the most abstract, so it is
the most <u>practical</u> of all, for it
admits of <u>universal</u> <u>application</u> (my
emphasis).[68]

From this it should be obvious that my earlier use of
Urmson is by no means arbitrary. That Thoreau was still
concerned about duty in 1853 has been seen in his
thoughts when in the Maine woods. The skinning of the
moose was a "tragical business" that "destroyed the

pleasure of my adventure."[69]  It should be remembered
from __Walden__ that Thoreau rightly noticed that his own
practice was logically irrelevant to the truth of his
vegetarian claims.  But the "murder of the moose" in __The__
__Maine__ __Woods__ is especially painful to Thoreau because he
tasted the meat himself.  He nonetheless longed to be
"living like a philosopher on the fruits of the earth."
Elsewhere he describes eating birds and squirrels as
tragic, disgusting, and miserable.[70]

Some might allege that Thoreau __must__ be
supererogatory in his vegetarianism in that he also
disdained coffee and tea.  But Thoreau's references to
these substances[71] are clearly part of his asceticism or
his desire to have a clear head.  There is no indication
that he sees tea leaves or coffee beans themselves as
loci of concern, as is the case with cows and pigs.
Also, Thoreau's alleged vegetarian supererogation may be
seen by some as analogous to his attitude toward sex:
"Chastity is the flowering of man."[72]  If Thoreau had
said "celibacy," then the charge of supererogation would
be hard to refute, because if celibacy were a duty for
all, the human race would soon be extinct.  Perhaps
because Thoreau himself was celibate, many have read
"celibacy" instead of "chastity" here.  In any event,

even if Thoreau was supererogatory in other areas, it is
not necessarily the case that his vegetarianism was
supererogatory.

If Singer is correct, now that racism and sexism
have finally been exposed as moral failings after
thousands of years of Western civilization, perhaps now
is as good a time as any to search for the roots of
"speciesism." Those who make this effort will have to
take Thoreau seriously. For example:

> ...man is the fiercest and cruelest
> animal....How meanly and grossly do
> we deal with nature!...We do not
> suspect how much might be done to
> improve our relation with animated
> nature; what kindness and refined
> courtesy there might be.[73]

Or again, there are continents and seas in the moral
world yet unexplored, and each person is an isthmus to
that world, but:

> How worn and dusty, then, must be
> the highways of the world, how deep
> the ruts of tradition and
> conformity![74]

Platonists have done little to cause the meat-
eating rut, as opposed to Aristotelians or most modern
philosophers. As we have seen, the two great followers
of Plato in late antiquity, Porphyry and Iamblichus,
were two most important influences on Thoreau's
vegetarianism, with Pythagoras also playing a significant role. The greatest neoplatonist, Plotinus, also
was a vegetarian. It is no mere coincidence that Plato
himself was enamored of vegetarianism. As in Chapter
Three with respect to dipolar theism, if Plato were in
favor of vegetarianism it would make perfect sense that
Plotinus, Porphyry, and Iamblichus were vegetarians, and
hence would make understandable Thoreau's own beliefs.
Further, we should not rule out the possibility that
Thoreau's own Platonic attitude toward animals also came
from Plato directly.

Was Plato a vegetarian? This question has seldom
been asked, and perhaps for some good reasons. There
are certain passages in Plato where it is clear that we
have no duties toward animals. Johannes Haussleiter
cites these passages, and reaches the conclusion that
Plato was not convinced by any of the arguments for
vegetarianism offered in antiquity.[75] But the
relationship between Plato and vegetarian thought is far

more complex than Haussleiter indicates.

There was a pervasive sense in ancient Greek
culture that the past was better than the present.  At
times this belief took the form of a golden age of
perfection in which vegetarianism was practiced.[76]
Plato appeals to the myth of the ages in the Republic
(415A).  The person fit to rule, the philosopher, has
some gold; the guardians are to be of silver stock,
while in the producing class are to be found bronze and
iron.  Plato uses these metals as exemplifications of
what would happen in history if any one of these groups
ruled.  Complete peace and moral progress are only
possible in a golden age dominated by philosophers.  How
does all of this relate to the issue of vegetarianism?
Plato, it is clear, believed that at least some of the
ancients were vegetarians; we learn this through the
speech of the Athenian in the Laws (782).  The question
is whether Plato's belief in the golden philosophers
corresponds to his awareness of vegetarianism.  The
needed connection is found in the Statesman (269-274),
in the famous myth of cosmic reversal.  Here it can be
seen that those living in the age of Cronus were
vegetarians.

The age of Cronus was one of perfection. Human beings did not even have to plan or govern the universe. Tutelary deities or daemons did that by acting as shepherds to their human flock. There was neither savagery nor preying of creature on creature. Human beings had fruit without stint from trees and bushes. When destiny (heimarmene) took control of the world, chaos ensued and Zeus took over. The animal paradise of the golden age and a pastoral vocabulary gave way to violence to animals and a political vocabulary. Two inferences can be made: (1) The point to the story of the ages in the Republic (that Plato is imagining what history would be like if golden types-philosophers ruled), when joined with the evidence of the Statesman (that those in the golden race under Cronus were vegetarians) allows the inference that philosophers should be vegetarians. (2) However, as I have argued elsewhere,[77] because the point to the myth of cosmic reversal in the Statesman is that the ideal universe under Cronus has never existed in the physical realm any more than the Republic has, vegetarianism also seems to function as an ideal background or a paradigm against which judgments of actual eating practices are to be made. This sounds so much like Thoreau. Further, in the Laws (713) an analogy is drawn between Cronus's daemons and the human beings they rule, on the one hand, and human shepherds and the animals they tend, on the other. Dominion is not a license for eating (another Thoreauvian commonplace), in that it would be unfathomable for Cronus's helpers to eat human beings just because they were superior in intelligence to those human beings.

Given Plato's belief that an ideal rule would be one of concern toward animals, it is curious that he so easily accepts the practice of meat-eating. He does not condemn hunting and butchering as arts practiced in order to get food (Statesman 228E), nor does he object to the raising of livestock for consumption (Laws 847E). The pleasure that one has when eating (Greater Hippias 298E) seems to include the eating of animal flesh. Meat seems to be a wholesome food (Laws 667B), especially recommended for athletes (Republic 404C). An apparent contradiction faces us. On the one hand, Plato looks at vegetarianism as an ideal worthy of striving for; on the other, he quite easily accepts less than ideal eating habits. But this situation is not so much a contradiction as a particular instance of the general theory-praxis tension in Plato's thought, exemplified in

the two glances motif treated in Chapter Two in a
general way, in Chapter Three with respect to divine
transcendence and immanence, and now here in Chapter
Four with respect to higher laws dealing with animals
lower than human beings. When it comes to eating it
seems that Plato somewhat abandons his ideal in order to
concentrate on what he thought were more important
problems regarding justice to human beings in "this"
world. But he did not completely abandon the ideal.
Likewise, Thoreau did not abandon the ideal by making
concessions to illiterate hunters and Indians.

Three key texts force me to keep alive the
possibility that Plato was a vegetarian, or at the very
least, was supportive of vegetarian thought. The first
is in the Republic (369D-373E). Here Socrates suggests,
immediately after proposing the creation of the
Republic, that the first and chief need of such a city
is food: no small honor! Division of labor will
produce not only food (barley meal, wheat flour, cakes),
but enough food for a feast: relishes like salt,
olives, cheese, onions, and greens; and desserts of
figs, chick-peas, beans, myrtle berries, and acorns.
These are foods of health and peace (presumably, peace
with animals). Then Socrates is asked what foods would

be eaten if he were not founding a Republic but a less
than ideal city. The reply: the delicacies (tragemata)
that are now in use. These presumably include the
sweetmeats (because this less than ideal city is to be a
city of "pigs," one should ask whether pigs eat these)
that are noticeably absent from the diet of the citizens
of Socrates' ideal city. That the Republic was to be a
vegetarian city is one of the best kept secrets in the
history of ideas, but is it hard to imagine Thoreau
noticing this fact? I think not.

The second text is from Plato's last dialogue, the
Laws (781E-783B), showing that this problem spans the
different periods in Plato's career. Here the Athenian
makes it clear that the history of human institutions
including the history of eating habits is immeasurably
long. Every sort of taste in meat and drink has been
exhibited in the past. This leads one to wonder about
the Greek practice of anthropophagy, as Thoreau himself
wondered. Some people not only avoided such brutality,
but also abstained from oxen and other more "acceptable"
flesh. To eat such flesh was criminal, and to sacrifice
it to the gods was a pollution. Cakes and meal soaked
in honey were considered much more pure. These unnamed
people, who insisted on universal vegetarianism like the

Orphics, can be none other than Thoreau's favorites the
Pythagoreans. Now comes the key point. Clinias adds
(with no objection from the Athenian, that is, Plato)
that this vegetarianism is a widely current and highly
credible tradition (kai sphorda legomena te eikekas kai
pisteuesthai pithana). As in the Republic, the prime
need of human beings is food, and vegetarianism is a
current, highly credible way of meeting that need.

Finally, there is the Epinomis (974D-975B). Here
the Athenian (again, Plato) holds that some people may
have been considered wise long ago, but are not so
considered now. Vegetarians are not in this category.
The legend of these people (the Pythagoreans) has it
that they put a check on the devouring of flesh. Their
rule still has a blessing of the first order from the
Athenian. The eating of barley and wheat is still
admirable. It may not in itself bring wisdom (but
neither the Pythagoreans nor Thoreau believed this
either), but such eating does show an attempt to become
virtuous. In the last analysis, Plato seems to tolerate
meat-eating in a way analogous to Pythagoras' tolerance
of the less rigorous practices of those who heard his
teachings but were not full members of his philosophical
society, the akousmatikoi; and analogous to Thoreau's

tolerance of meat-eating by the primitive inhabitants of wild regions.  None of these thinkers actually defends the practice of eating meat.  True philosophers, for Thoreau, should strive for the highest by being on the trail for a rarer game.[78]

NOTES: CHAPTER FOUR

[1]Anderson, p. 151.

[2]Rice, rye meal, apples, potatoes, corn, peas, turnips, molasses, salt, purslane, nuts, and berries (hardly a "scanty fare of vegetables," see _Walden_, p. 203). He also tasted, but did not like, cherries, and had a Pythagorean dislike of beans. See pp. 54, 59, 61, 114, 162, 173, 239.

[3]Anderson, pp. 152, 161.

[4]Seybold, p. 61. Why it is more likely that vegetarians be fanatics than meat-eaters is not made clear.

[5]Seybold, p. 61. Once again, why vegetarianism is more likely to be foolish than meat-eating is not stated.

[6]Joseph Jones, "Transcendental Grocery Bills: Thoreau's _Walden_ and Some Aspects of American Vegetarianism," _University of Texas Studies in English_ 36 (1957), p. 149. Those who see Thoreau's vegetarianism as inconsistent or indecisive include the following: Edward Wagenknecht, _Henry David Thoreau: What Manner of Man?_ (Amherst: University of Massachusetts Press, 1981), p. 21; and Frederick Garber, _Thoreau's Redemptive Imagination_ (New York: New York University Press, 1977). In this chapter I will try to

respond to these legitimate concerns.

[7]Jones, p. 154.

[8]Henry S. Salt, The Life of Henry David Thoreau
(1890), p. 166.

[9]Salt's work Animals' Rights has recently been
given a new edition (1980), with an introduction by
Peter Singer.

[10]Foerster, p. 36, records Alcott's implication
that vegetarianism is a Platonic and Pythagorean
tradition.

[11]J.O. Urmson, "Saints and Heroes," in Essays in
Moral Philosophy, ed. by A.I. Melden (Seattle:
University of Washington Press, 1958).

[12]Ibid., p. 198.

[13]Ibid., pp. 200-201.

[14]Not all supererogatory acts are heroic, however.
For example, someone voluntarily picking up litter that
other people have dropped. Further, I realize that a
full treatment of saintly acts would have to include
consideration of the motivation for such acts. The need
for the category of supererogatory acts is seen when we
try to place them elsewhere. They are certainly not
prohibited, nor are they duties. To say that they are
permissible leaves so much unexplained as to be

misleading.

[15]Urmson, p. 203.

[16]Ibid., p. 209.

[17]Ibid., p. 211.

[18]Ibid., p. 212.

[19]Ibid., p. 213.

[20]Pickard, p. 85.

[21]Ibid., p. 86.

[22]See Wolf, p. 92.

[23]Ralph Waldo Emerson, "Thoreau," in Selected Prose and Poetry, ed. by Reginald L. Cook (New York: Holt, Rinehart, and Winston, 1969), p. 259.

[24]Ibid., p. 260. The vegetarian metaphor in this quotation is significant and not just because Thoreau grew beans while at Walden Pond. When Emerson says, p. 251, that for Thoreau all diets are a small matter, he seems to be saying (like Anderson or Seybold) that at least Thoreau was not a fanatic reformer.

[25]Anderson, p. 24. Jones, p. 143.

[26]Walden, p. 218. Also see Journal, volume 2, p. 324, where Thoreau suggests that only the lean can do philosophy; those with "full orbed" bellies are not fit for it.

[27]Walden, p. 215.

[28]Ibid., p. 214.

[29]Anderson, p. 153.

[30]Cameron, _Transcendental Apprenticeship_, p. 117, alerts us to similarities between Greeks like Pythagoras and Indian philosophers on vegetarianism. Cameron cites extracts from Hugh Murray, _Historical and Descriptive Account of British India_ (New York: 1832). Wolf, p. 99, claims that Thoreau's vegetarianism had precedent in the Hindus and St. Paul, yet curiously does not mention Platonic influences. Also see "The Laws of Menu," in _Early Essays_, as well as "Sayings of Confucius." Perhaps this is the appropriate place to mention that Thoreau's classicism and his Orientalism are not necessarily mutually exclusive. In late antiquity there were significant points of interpenetration between Greek thought and Oriental thought. Plotinus, for example, went as far east as Persia, which, after the time of Alexander the Great had been a place where east met west. See Emile Brehier, _The Philosophy of Plotinus_ (Chicago: University of Chicago Press, 1958), Chapter VII.

[31]Jones, p. 146, quotes this Alcott as saying that the most serious objection to eating meat was "the moral insensibility which its familiar use involves." The

transcendentalists were not just food cranks, as Jones
sometimes suggests. Also see Louis B. Salomon, "The
Least-Remembered Alcott," New England Quarterly 34
(1961), pp. 87-93.

[32]Anderson, pp. 153-155. Also see Emerson,
"Thoreau," p. 256; and Salt, The Life, p. 167, where
Thoreau's Pythagorean charm with animals is discussed.
Anderson is one of the few scholars who have noticed the
central role of Porphyry and Iamblichus in "Higher
Laws." Seybold, p. 15, also documents the fact that
Thoreau read Porphyry and Iamblichus.

[33]On Porphyry see On Abstinence from Animal Food,
translated by Thomas Taylor (London: Centaur Press,
1965); on Iamblichus see Life of Pythagoras, translated
by Thomas Taylor (London: Valpy, 1818). The former is
a new edition of Taylor's translation. The most
scholarly edition is by Bouffartigue and Patillon,
Porphyre de l' abstinence (Paris: 1977), 3 volumes.
Again, see my "Vegetarianism and the Argument from
Marginal Cases in Porphyry," and The Philosophy of
Vegetarianism.

[34]Seybold, p. 61.

[35]See Anderson, pp. 153-155. On Socrates'
(Plato's) identification of himself with Apollo see

Phaedo (85A-B).

[36]Jeremy Bentham, The Principles of Morals and Legislation (1789), XVII, 1. Thoreau thinks that men and fish are much closer than most people think; it is too easy to spot the differences, but similarities are discovered through sympathy. See Journal, volume 2, p. 108.

[37]Peter Singer, Animal Liberation (New York: New York Review, 1975), p. 265.

[38]And we do surely want to protect these people, although not all of the Greeks did, as is evidenced by the practice of infanticide.

[39]Tom Regan, "Fox's Critique of Animal Liberation," Ethics 88 (January, 1978), pp. 126-133.

[40]Porphyry, III, 19-20.

[41]Walden, p. 212. Also, Thoreau criticizes those who think that a fish's weight is its only claim to fame, p. 184.

[42]Ibid., p. 175.

[43]Ibid., p. 214.

[44]Ibid., p. 9. Thoreau also makes it clear that human beings can adapt to more climates and circumstances than any other creatures, p. 63. He asks rhetorically, p. 166, "How, then, can our harvest fail?"

Only foolish unbelievers (and unscientific ones!) would
doubt that eating vegetables can be healthy, pp. 64-65.

[45]Ibid., p. 12.

[46]Ibid., p. 61.

[47]Ibid., p. 211.

[48]Ibid., pp. 213-214.

[49]Ibid., p. 211.

[50]Ibid., pp. 215-216. Thoreau believes it a
"divine suggestion" not to eat meat. In this belief he
follows Greeks like Plato; some Greeks did eat meat, but
only after the animal was killed as part of some
religious ritual, as Thoreau correctly notes; animals
were never mere things or commodities for the Greeks, as
they are on modern factory farms. See Journal, volume
2, pp. 175, 233-235. Even nations are ennobled by
protecting weaker species.

[51]Walden, p. 216. Reinforcing my suggestion that
Thoreau was a saint is p. 224, where the hermit opposes
fishing to heaven. Also on Thoreau's loss of respect
for himself when he fished see Journal, volume 2, p.
241.

[52]Walden, pp. 210, 216.

[53]Ibid., p. 218. It should be noticed that when
Thoreau was tempted to fish it was his philosophy, not

his feelings, which protested, p. 211.

[54]Ibid., p. 219.

[55]Ibid., p. 15.

[56]Ibid., p. 212. On p. 122 it appears that even the sheepdog mourns the slaughter of the sheep.

[57]Ibid., p. 216. Thoreau also thinks it important not to overwork animals, p. 157, nor to rob from birds' breasts to keep warm, p. 13. Yet another argument for vegetarianism is that eating meat inefficiently uses the earth's resources, hence leaving less for hungry human beings. Thoreau notices that the farmer must give most of his grain to his animals (victims), p. 63.

[58]Singer, p. 215.

[59]Walden, p. 302.

[60]Wolf, p. 106. Also see Walden, pp. 306, 308.

[61]Wolf, pp. 118, 148. For example, at one point Thoreau suggests that all matter can entertain "thought." If what Thoreau means is a primitive analogue to mind whereby subatomic particles "feel," then his position can be rationally defended. See Journal, volume 2, p. 146.

[62]Walden, p. 215. For the quote from Kohák above see The Embers and the Stars: A Philosophical Inquiry into the Moral Sense of Nature (Chicago: University of

Chicago Press, 1984), pp. 124-125.

[63]Ibid., p. 250. Singer traces what I have called
S2 "down" the scale of being (or better, the scale of
becoming) to shrimp and oysters, which constitute a grey
area between plants, which do not have S2 for all we can
tell, and animals or fish, which obviously do have S2.
In Walden, p. 240, Thoreau shows that wasps also are in
a grey area when he is reluctant to kill them unless
they prove a bother. On p. 273 Thoreau shows an
awareness of degrees of nobility among animals.

[64]Orientals and Greeks who believed in
transmigration held that animals were, or will be, human
beings, and the same is true of plants. There is a
famous story in Diogenes Laertius (VIII, 36) of
Pythagoras asking a man to discontinue beating a dog
because he recognized the voice of a deceased friend in
the yelp of the animal. The voice could just as well,
on these grounds, have come from a dogwood. It must be
admitted that Thoreau refers to the killing of an animal
as effecting its transmigration, Walden, p. 59.

[65]Walden, pp. 283-284. Thoreau's scale of being
also includes gradations in the plant world, for
example, "nobler plants." See p. 15; also see Walter
Harding, The Variorum Walden, p. 270, note 40. But

since these plant gradations do not involve S2 they do
not affect vegetarianism. Regarding the supposed
necessity of eating meat, Thoreau finds it significant
(Walden, p. 215) that some insects are furnished with
organs of feeding that they do not use. It is good to
consider the diet of the Indians in determining what
foods are really necessary, p. 143. Also, only
necessary work should be imposed on animals, as opposed
to work done for the luxury or sport of human beings, p.
56.

[66]Walden, pp. 210, 217. I have greatly benefited
from Thomas Altherr's paper, " 'Chaplain to the
Hunters': Henry David Thoreau's Ambivalence Toward
Hunting." Also see Walden, p. 161. In a very telling
passage Thoreau complains about the stench of Concord's
slaughterhouse; a simpler and truer life would have
prevented this. See Journal, volume 2, p. 125.
Finally, see Robert Epstein, "A Benefactor to His Race:
Thoreau's 'Higher Laws' and the Heroics of
Vegetarianism," Between the Species 1 (Summer, 1985),
pp. 23-28, where a fine treatment of Thoreau's
vegetarianism can be found. Epstein thinks Thoreau's
heroics largely consists in the willingness to let
nature alone. Anderson, p. 151, notices that Thoreau's

development from earth to heaven, or from wildness to virtue, cannot take a shortcut by denying the animal in him, for then he would land in the limbo of mere civilization.

[67]The Maine Woods, ed. by Joseph Moldenhauer (Princeton: Princeton University Press, 1972), p. 99. In Walden, Thoreau's friend the Canadian woodsman, who was a great consumer of meat, is an example of a primitive meat-eater whom Thoreau could tolerate, p. 145. Nevertheless, those who tred the forest for meat not only will digest with pain but also deserve to be called Troglidites. See Journal, volume 2, p. 166, cf. pp. 136-137.

[68]Early Essays, pp. 106-108. Also see pp. 31-32, 97-98.

[69]The Maine Woods, pp. 115-122, 135, 143.

[70]A Week, pp. 223-224. In Walden, p. 218, Thoreau refers to turtle and muscrat meat as "savage tid-bits." And on p. 204 he says that chickens are too humanized (that is, sentient) to roast well.

[71]Walden, p. 217.

[72]Ibid., pp. 219-220.

[73]Reform Papers, p. 22. Also see Singer, pp. 1-27. And Journal, volume 2, p. 146, where Thoreau holds that

philosophers should eat in "advance" of their

generation.

[74]Walden, p. 323 and p. 321. Also see Reform

Papers, p. 194.

[75]Johannes Haussleiter, Der Vegetarismus in der

antike (Berlin: Topelmann, 1935). Again, see my "Was

Plato a Vegetarian?," and The Philosophy of

Vegatarianism.

[76]Those who attest to the belief that "originally"

people were vegetarian include Hesiod, Empedocles,

Theophrastus, Dicaerchus, Ephorus, Aratus, Diodorus

Siculus, Ovid--whom Thoreau refers to several times,

Plotinus, and Porphyry. Texts where Thoreau himself

refers to the golden age are easy to find. At one point

he equates the antediluvian age with Plato's predecessor

Thales. See Journal, volume 2, p. 72.

[77]Plato's Philosophy of History, Chapter Seven.

[78]Journal, volume 2, p. 249.

# CHAPTER FIVE: THOREAU AND THE PLATONIC FUNCTIONS OF LANGUAGE

"Plato is philosophy, and philosophy, Plato."[1] So hyperbolized Emerson in his essay on Plato published in 1850, during the height of Thoreau's writing career. We have seen in Chapters One and Two that Thoreau also thought very highly of Plato, and in Chapters Two, Three, and Four it has been made clear that Thoreau was a Platonist in ways that scholars have not previously mentioned. Could it be that Emerson had Thoreau in mind when he said: "Out of Plato come all things that are still written and debated among men of thought" (my emphasis)?[2] Despite the intellectual differences between Emerson and Thoreau, did Emerson ever meet a more thoughtful person than Thoreau? Or again, Emerson claims that "Plato seems to a reader in New England an American genius."[3] We should remember that Emerson once said that there was no truer American than Thoreau; could the New England reader Emerson refers to be Thoreau? Such speculation, although idle, is nonetheless extremely interesting when Emerson's particular approach to Plato in his essay is carefully considered.

Emerson's thesis in his essay is that the genius of
Plato consists in his having a "balanced soul" that can
"enhance the energy of each" pole in what I have called
dipolar contrasts,[4] among which Emerson mentions the
following:

| | |
|---|---|
| unity | variety |
| identity | diversity |
| oneness | manyness |
| sameness | otherness |
| cause | effect |
| mind | nature |
| Europe | Asia |

Emerson again hyperbolizes when he says: "Every great
artist has been such by synthesis"[5] of these two poles.
But he nonetheless points us in the right direction
toward an understanding of Thoreau, at least, if not all
great artists. Like Plato, Thoreau was interested in
"mounting into heaven" while "diving into the pit."[6]
Yet neither Plato nor Thoreau so much synthesize these
two poles as shows the place and importance of each.
Thoreau also demonstrates how the pole on the right side
symbolizes the concrete cosmos out of which can be
abstracted the immaterial reality symbolized by the left
side.

To Platonize, for Emerson, is quite simply to give a spiritual, ethical, or intellectual expression to every truth.[7] It is to exhibit an ulterior end which is yet legitimate to the natural fact in question. Given this definition of what it means to Platonize, who could doubt that Thoreau was a Platonist? A list Emerson makes of the everyday examples used in Socrates' and Plato's own philosophical pursuits makes one think of, say, Thoreau's desire to understand the morality of war through a dispute between red and black ants. Socrates and Plato discussed cocks, quails, soup-pans, sycamore-spoons, mares, puppies, pitchers, soup-ladles, cooks, criers, potters, and horse doctors.[8] (Emerson ignores the section of the _Parmenides_ where the significance of mud and hair are considered.) "Orators and polite conversers" disdain these sources of wisdom, but Thoreau knew how to decipher the philosophical significance of an owl or ice or clouds. In contrast to some contemporary, rather popular, theories of literature fostered by the deconstructionists, there is no isolated world within words for Plato or Thoreau. Rather, their poetic gifts themselves are instruments used for an ulterior purpose.[9] Simply put, words are Platonized. This is quite obvious to Emerson. Speaking of Plato he says:

> He is intellectual in his aim; and
> __therefore__, in expression, literary
> (my emphasis).[10]

It is unthinkable to Emerson that words be an exception
to the rest of reality, even apparently insignificant
reality. That is, words themselves have their place in
the architecture of the Platonic universe. Like __eros__ in
the __Symposium__, they act as "daemonic" mediators between,
as Thoreau would put it, this world and the eternal.

One of the functions of language is to slow down
the "modern man," who does not even have time to
remember his ignorance, which, in Socratic fashion, is
required for human growth.[11] Thoreau is quite explicit
that we should obey the precept of the "old philosopher"
(Socrates) to "Explore thyself," to explore our own
higher latitudes.[12] Because modern philosophers do not
use their words to solve some of the practical problems
of life (for example, how to live, how to eat, et al.),
Thoreau insists that today there are only professors of
philosophy, but not true philosophers. The real
philosopher lives simply in all respects, and hence must
live and eat in ways unlike his contemporaries.[13] Greek

philosophers like Plato knew this, but it is not so obvious that mid-nineteenth century or late-twentieth century philosophers (mostly language analysts) know it.

Thoreau is under no illusion that we will be likely to have a whole nation of philosophers,[14] all cooperating together. Unfortunately, human cooperation as it is is largely superficial; true harmony is like the inaudible (to most human beings) sounds of Pythagoras's planetary spheres; and only some sounds in this world effect a "vibration of the universal lyre."[15] Even when human beings do not create cacophony they do not necessarily exist in harmony. Like isolated, mutually exclusive notes, thirty people can crowd into a room without getting near each other.[16]

Language, as used in the newspapers Thoreau loathed, often degenerates into the "mere smoke of opinion,"[17] the realm of doxa in Plato's cave and in the divided line of the Republic. "Fix not thy heart on that which is transitory."[18] Integral to Walden's structure is a Platonic pair of glances in which the upward glance inspires Thoreau to claim that:

Every man is tasked to make his

life, even in its details, worthy of

the contemplation of his most

elevated and critical hour (my

emphasis).[19]

No doubt this is difficult (but not impossible) to do in

the "dark unfathomed mammoth cave of this world," an

obvious allusion to Plato.[20]

Poetry (that is, true speech) would "resound along

the streets" if we realized:

...that only great and worthy things

have any permanent and absolute

existence,--that petty fears and

petty pleasures are but the shadow

of the reality....By...consenting to

be deceived by shows, men establish

and confirm their daily life of

routine and habit every where, which

still is built on purely illusory

foundations (my emphasis).[21]

As is made obvious in so many of Thoreau's allusions to

Plato, Thoreau is what contemporary philosophers (with

their architectural metaphors) would call a

foundationalist, not a deconstructionist. A Platonic

foundationalist at that. In eternity there is "indeed something true and sublime"; the purpose of philosophic, religious, and poetic language is to speak properly about "reality" (Thoreau's emphasis), even if this requires us to:

> ...work and wedge our feet downward
> through the mud and slush of
> opinion, and prejudice, and
> tradition, and delusion, and
> appearance, that alluvian which
> covers the globe![22]

Time's current slides away; eternity remains; hence we must learn our alphabet all over again.[23]

As in Plato, however, in Thoreau time can image eternity. We are mortal, but to the extent that we can focus on truth--seen as the correspondence of words to reality--we are immortal.[24] That is, truth can be found by focusing on eternity or by abstracting from temporal experience those features that resemble eternity (which requires that an exacting attention be paid to the features of temporal experience). Even a dreamlike, angling metaphor can help us learn the truth about ourselves as mediators between two worlds:

It was very queer, especially in
dark nights, when your thoughts had
wandered to vast and cosmogonal
themes in other spheres, to feel
this faint jerk, which came to
interrupt your dreams and link you
to Nature again. It seemed as if I
might next cast my line upward into
the air, as well as downward into
this element which was scarcely more
dense. Thus I caught two fishes as
it were with one hook.[25]

Walden Pond itself is "intermediate in its nature
between land and sky"; it is "God's drop."[26]

At times Thoreau speaks as if we should use our
understanding of higher reality to guide our practical
affairs. For example:

I believe that every man who has
ever been earnest to preserve his
higher or poetic faculties in the
best condition has been particularly
inclined to abstain from animal
food.[27]

But at other times Thoreau implies that it is the
natural world that we must use to guide our
understanding of the eternal.  In point of fact the two
processes interpenetrate.  Is this not the point to
Thoreau's story about John Farmer, a story which occurs
at the very end of "Higher Laws"?:

> A voice said to him,--Why do you
> stay here and live this mean moiling
> life, when a glorious existence is
> possible for you?...All that he
> could think of was to practise some
> new austerity, to let his mind
> descend into his body and redeem it,
> and treat himself with ever
> increasing respect.[28]

Nikos Kazantzakis' great hero Zorba may be of help here,
especially when he speaks to his boss about life as a
process of transubstantiation.  That is, the bread which
Thoreau extols is the raw material out of which thoughts
and spirituality are made:

> Tell me what you do with the food
> you eat, and I'll tell you who you
> are.  Some turn their food into fat
> and manure, some into work and good

humor, and others, I'm told, into
God. So there must be three sorts
of men. I'm not one of the worst,
boss, nor yet one of the best. I'm
somewhere between the two. What I
eat I turn into work and good
humor....As for you, boss...I think
you do your level best to turn what
you eat into God.[29]

John Farmer and Thoreau are like the boss. It should be
noted that liturgical transubstantiation (like
creation--"God said 'Let there be light' ") occurs
through words being spoken. Likewise, we eat so as to
transform matter into spiritual thoughts. Or as Thoreau
implies in the John Farmer story, through austerity we
are to redeem our bodies and all natural bodies, and to
treat them with respect. Asceticism is not always the
exclusively otherworldly activity many assume it to
be.[30] Just as food is instrumental in achieving an
understanding of eternity, so is language, although
language obviously is a more complicated sort of
instrument. There is no necessary conflict between
literary creativity and subservience to a divine ideal.
In Thoreau's conception of things we can freely and

imaginatively build a poetic stairway to heaven, just as the earth, fertilized by dead human flesh, can push its green blade to eternity.[31]

Thoreau laments: "There is an incessant influx of novelty into the world, and yet we tolerate incredible dulness."[32] If we do not appreciate the higher (Platonic or neoplatonic) realities it is not because we do not have the time. Thoreau thinks his experiment at Walden has proven this. But "this restless, nervous, bustling, trivial Nineteenth Century"[33] hardly seems to have the time to read Plato carefully (remember Thoreau's remark about Plato's long, difficult sentences[34]) or even to read him at all. When one looks at the twentieth century one realizes that the situation has not improved. Thoreau's advice to the nineteenth and twentieth century individual is simply simplicity:

> ...he will live with the license of
> a higher order of beings. In
> proportion as he simplifies his
> life, the laws of the universe will
> appear less complex, and solitude
> will not be solitude, nor poverty
> poverty, nor weakness weakness. If
> you have built castles in the air,

> your work need not be lost; that is
> where they should be. Now put the
> foundations under them.[35]

In that Thoreau refers to "laws of the universe" in this
quotation, one understands that what he means by putting
foundations in is to discover the foundations already
there.

Thoreau's classical conception of the orderliness
and beauty of the world, and of the functions of
language to depict that orderliness and beauty, and his
desire to exhort us to take time to see them, are
opposed by the language of we moderns, who "love
eloquence for its own sake."[36] Actually, this latter
view of language is an old one, too, as is evidenced in
the mouths of the sophists in several of Plato's
dialogues. No doubt Thoreau thought of government
officials in his day as contemporary Hippiases or Ions.
Luckily, even in this world we do not have to think a
majority of the time about the words of politicians
(even if we do have to think about their words some of
the time, and react to them as well); we should spend a
greater portion of our time thinking about the words of
those thinkers who "legislate for all time."[37] Who
could now doubt that Thoreau thought Plato to be one of

these thinkers?

There is an alternation, however, in Thoreau
between a Platonic and neoplatonic conception of
language.  In Plato's Seventh Letter even he is
sceptical of the ability of words to carry truth,
whereas in the myth concerning the origin of writing in
the Phaedrus only the written word receives criticism.
Generally speaking, however, Plato prefers spoken
language, which remains close to thought, and written
language which remains as close as posible to the spoken
dialectic of the agora (as in his dialogue style).  We
have seen Thoreau admit that he was a mystic,[38] hence it
is not surprising that at times he says religion is that
which is never spoken.[39]  At these points he appears as
a neoplatonic mystic, sceptical of the value of language
regarding God.  But as Hartshorne has ably shown,[40]
mysticism can mean either:  (1) immediate experience of
God, or (2) the belief that this experience and God are
ineffable.  Thoreau gives eivdence of being a mystic in
both senses.  In the former sense he can talk about God
without neoplatonic scepticism concerning language about
God.  It would certainly be paradoxical to think that
God could only be affirmed indirectly, especially if God
is ubiquitous.  Data that are only sometimes present

(for example, redness or pain) are easier to detect than those which are always there (for example, Sl). Thoreau is explicitly _aware_ of experiencing what all human beings experience implicitly, and he _tells_ us so (see my treatments of Thoreau's panpsychism in Chapters Three and Four). "With an eye made quiet by the power of harmony and the deep power of joy," says Wordsworth in his poem about Tintern Abbey, the mystic sees "into the life of things."

But what is the function of language for the interpreter?, and for the interpreter of Thoreau in particular? Susan Sontag--one of the most important critics of interpretation, and one of the clearest--who generally is an opponent to the theory of art as representation (and hence to Platonism), nonetheless admits in her review of Rolf Hochhuth's The Deputy that:

> Some art--but not all--elects as its
> central purpose to tell the truth;
> and it must be judged by its
> fidelity to the truth, and by the
> relevance of the truth which it
> tells.[41]

This states precisely my assumptions throughout this book. Nietzsche's dictum, "There are no facts, only interpretations"[42] (which seems to be the core insight in the theory of literature developed by Jacques Derrida and other deconstructionists) is a canard when applied to Thoreau, who so earnestly and consistently--albeit in a dipolar way--states what he believes to be the truth about ourselves and our relationships with God and nature. Using Sontag's language, what I have used in this book is "the old style of interpretation," prominent in which is a "piety towards the troublesome text." Only it is not so much Thoreau's text that I find troublesome, as the failure of previous inter- preters to notice Platonism as an important conceptual feature of Thoreau's writing. I admit that any interpreter, even one who does not erase or rewrite the text, alters it. My reader's job is to determine if I have, and the degree to which I have, done an injustice to Thoreau by my alteration. My own sense is that I am "reading off a sense that is already there."[43] There is one point that Sontag (and the deconstructionists) surely have right: that the interpreter should not try to end discourse about an author with a totalitarian- like braggadocio that seems to say that "This is what

Thoreau is <u>really</u> about." My purpose is the exact
opposite: to complicate discourse about Thoreau, or
better, to enrich it by calling attention to a side of
Thoreau largely ignored in previous treatments, even the
best ones. Hence, I escape most of Sontag's criticisms
of interpretation.

· "The modern style of interpretation" is Sontag's
real enemy because of its "open aggressiveness" toward
the text, its attempt to get "behind" the text "to find
a sub-text which is the true one." (She seems to have
certain Freudian,[44] Marxist, and structuralist critics
in mind.) My thesis, however, is that we need not get
"behind" Thoreau's works to see that he was a Platonist;
we need only to read carefully the texts in which
Thoreau cites or alludes to Plato, or consider the books
that Thoreau read to see some obvious similarities (and
causal connections) between ancient wisdom and
Thoreauvian exhortation. But according to Sontag, today
is a time:

> ...when the project of
> interpretation is largely
> reactionary, stifling. Like the
> fumes of the automobile and of heavy
> industry which befoul the urban

atmosphere, the effusion of
interpretations of art today poisons
our sensibilities ....interpretation
is the revenge of the intellect upon
art.[45]

Note Sontag's comparison of automobile fumes (which
Thoreau would find an abomination) with the forces of
reaction ("the modern style of interpretation"). I have
tried to show that Thoreau truly is a breath of fresh
air, as is Plato. And even if Thoreau sometimes shares
Plato's disdain for government by the masses,[46] he does
not knowingly give his support to reactionary forces.
Nor (thank goodness!) do I.

Sontag also (rightfully) bemoans the fact that
modern interpretation "tames the work of art.
Interpretation makes art manageable, conformable."[47]
But I prefer to leave Thoreau wild, outside of
contemporary society's and contemporary academe's (cf.
Plato's original Academy) neatly tended gardens. In
these institutions civil disobedience is frowned upon
(yet as I write the United States is still slaughtering
people south of the border, this time in El Salvador and
Nicaragua, as opposed to Mexico); the issue of God is
largely irrelevant or treated in an undialectical,

superficial way; and vegetarianism is mostly a source of mild amusement. I have been civilly disobedient; I am a theist, and a vegetarian to boot. Does this sound too bold[48] or vain, or unprofessional for an academic to admit in a scholarly book? If so, then perhaps we need to read Thoreau once again, this time taking him at his word. As before, I think I have avoided most of Sontag's criticisms of interpretation.

The most successful of recent interpreters of Thoreau at doing justice both to Thoreau's language and to Thoreau's debt to Plato is Stanley Cavell. Concomitant with Cavell's analysis of the development of Walden's purpose through words, sentences, and "portions" is an analysis of Thoreau's classicism. Cavell is surely correct in noting: "The very greatest masterpieces, when one is fresh from them, are apt to seem neglected."[49] And what has often been neglected in Thoreau is his "extremity" of praise for the classics, his "devotion" to the ancients.[50] For example, like Socrates Thoreau is often prompted to philosophize through nothing other than his neighbor's using language foolishly.[51] Hence, Thoreau tries to redeem language by writing a new classic which will revitalize ancient wisdom.[52] Cavell is on stronger ground here than many suppose. Thoreau himself speaks of the classics as "the noblest recorded thoughts of man."[53] Nonetheless, "A living dog is better than a dead lion."[54] That is, Plato's leonine nobility can live only through our canine efforts. A dog is our best friend, they say. But only thought can enable us to appreciate what is lasting in Plato. The affections, like water, can easily turn putrid; grand thoughts, like ice, retain a frozen sweetness.[55]

Cavell also notices that for Thoreau human beings live in two worlds, but he thinks the two worlds "show little relation to one another."[56] It is paradoxical for Cavell that what is nearest to us is also the farthest away.[57] But this is a paradox only on the Kantian or Wittgensteinian grounds that Cavell often presupposes. I hope my treatment of Thoreau's dipolar theism and his higher laws regarding lowly animals has alleviated the paradox somewhat. What leads Cavell astray in Walden is the following pair: "the depth of the book's depressions and the height of its elevation."[58] To assume that the two are mutually exclusive is to fail to consider that they may be the result of looking in opposite directions from one consistent position. For a Platonist, looking up is always elevating; simultaneously looking down is not always depressing, but it can be so.

What is enticing in Cavell's book is the fact that he constantly flirts with the idea that Thoreau was a Platonist. Our choice as human beings, Cavell says, is whether we will be "metaphysicians or manikins."[59] The first step in our metaphysical education is to notice the strangeness of our lives,[60] say the strangeness of our killing and eating animals with S2. (Plato's concern for harmony of soul does not necessarily pre-clude this pedagogical "doubleness," as Cavell implies.[61]) Further along the road comes saintliness, and Cavell is right in saying that even if Thoreau did not philosophize in the agora like Socrates, or in the Academy like Plato, he nonetheless moved only one mile from neighbors so that he could still listen and talk to them and be a "visible saint."[62] To be a false saint is hypocritical, but even true saints seem to hypocrites to have bad manners.[63] Here Socrates and Thoreau are as one. It was hypocrisy that Plato fled, not the natural world or his fellow citizens.[64]

At present we have "an impoverished idea of philosophy"[65] and of life. Thoreau's value as a philosopher lies not in logical precision (although he was by no means illogical); rather, he is primarily interested in orienting us properly regarding the big questions in life.[66] By now it should not be surprising that the following should be said about Walden's concern for the big questions:

> It is not the first time in our
> literature, and it will not be the
> last, in which society is viewed as
> a prison. As with Plato's cave, the
> path out is as arduous as the one
> the Republic requires of
> philosophers--and like the Republic,
> Walden is presided over by the sun,
> and begins with a stripping away of
> false necessities.[67]

Has anyone, even Cavell, ever done justice to the last line of Walden? This line strikes blindness in the unenlightened eye: "The sun is but a morning star."[68] In order to escape the cave to see the morning star it is not necessary to view language as an ornament to thought, as icing on the cake. Rather, language is the incarnation of thought. One four-term analogy is to be

rejected and another adopted if we are to understand
Thoreau's view of language.[69]  The misleading analogy
suggests:

        expression : meaning :: garb : body

As Thoreau suggests, beware of any occupation which
requires new clothes. More helpful is this:

        expression : meaning :: body : soul

In a Platonic view of language words do not merely
mirror reality.[70]  They reach beneath the transient
surface (or grasp above it) to touch the enduring
reality.  Metaphors do not describe facts but evoke a
sense; they evoke a meaning which precedes words.
Thoreau was astute enough to realize that philosophy is
not a techne which encodes data; it needs similes and
metaphors, as Plato better than any philosopher
illustrates.  Like amphibians we emerge from our aqueous
caves in search of the sun; like lightning God shines
the way.

    For Thoreau spoken language is as transient as the
shadows on the back wall of the cave, but "books must be
read as deliberately and reservedly as they were
written."[71]  Plato's works have long since outlasted the
Greek armies, yet his dialogues are as young as a
sunrise.  Godlike individuals, who form an invisible

upper class in every society, realize this. But these
individuals often have a difficult time finding each
other, hence Thoreau is often chagrined that no one
reads the best books: there is no one to talk to about
the Greek authors.[72] "I am infinitely more interested
in the old books than in the new." This is because the
ancient authors give us the most valuable monuments of
all time: "Only they talk of forgetting the ancients who
never knew them."[73] Our reading should be heroic by
catching but a glimmering of Plato's unexhausted
hieroglyphics, but for now we must bolster ourselves
with the realization that the portico of Greek
philosophy is still frequented by some (think of
Emerson). Go where you will, someone, most likely
Plato, has been there before.[74] In Wordsworthian
fashion, Thoreau's motto could well have been:

> We will grieve not, rather find
>
> Strength in what remains behind.

The point is that the search for Walden's bottom
(that is, the intellectual foundation for Thoreau's
universe) is not quite the Holy Grail that some make it
out to be. Walter Benn Michaels[75] suggests that
interpretations of Walden (but curiously not "Civil
Disobedience") are "inevitably arbitrary," and

constitute a "literary anarchy" because of the
contradictions Thoreau throws before us regarding the
foundations of his worldview.  Michaels is quite right
in saying that Walden Pond is quite deep, and indeed
there are a few false bottoms often touched by students
who read Thoreau for the first time, like the banal
comment that Thoreau was a hermit.  But what
contradictions does Thoreau pose to justify the claim
that it is theoretically impossible to find Thoreauvian
foundations?  Thoreau himself explicitly tells us how
deep the pond is.  And Michaels alerts us to the passage
where Thoreau exhorts us to:

> ...settle ourselves, and work and
> wedge our feet downward through the
> mud and slush of opinion, and
> prejudice, and tradition, and
> delusion, and appearance, that
> alluvion which covers the
> globe...through church and state,
> through poetry and philosophy and
> religion, till we come to a hard
> bottom and rocks in place, which we
> can call reality, and say, This is,
> and no mistake; and then begin,

having a <u>point</u> <u>d</u>' <u>appri</u>...a place

where you might found a wall or a

state.[76]

Yet against this already cited passage Michaels sees the
following text as the other player in Thoreau's zero-sum
game, where one passage can win only if the other loses;
that is, he sees these two pasages as mutually
exclusive:

There is a solid bottom everywhere.
We read that the traveller asked the
boy if the swamp before him had a
hard bottom. The boy replied that
it had. But presently the
traveller's horse sank in up to the
girths, and he observed to the boy,
"I thought you said that this bog
had a hard bottom." "So it has,"
answered the latter, "but you have
not got half way to it yet." So it
is with the bogs and quicksands <u>of</u>
<u>society</u>.[77]

My emphasis, of course. Wherein lies the
contradiction?, and where is the evidence that we will
die trying to find the bottom like the traveler?
Thoreau himself says that an "old boy" can find it.

My treatment of Thoreau and Plato in Chapters Two,
Three, and Four of this book, and Emerson's treatment of
Plato mentioned earlier in this chapter, should at least
offer some aperture of hope that the eternal and the
temporal, divine transcendence and immanence, and
saintliness and a concern for animals are not
necessarily contradictory. What is not often noticed in
some deconstructionist treatments of great writers is
that if "literary anarchy" were the case not only could
we not (nor could Thoreau) state the truth with any
degree of certainty, we could not even objectively state
what was false. Falsification with assurance (for
example, my scratching my head is not the cause of the
earth rotating on its axis) presupposes that the state
of affairs in question is in conflict with some stable
reality which acts as a standard. (On deconstructionist
grounds we could say only that it does not seem that my
scratching my head causes the earth to rotate.)
Moreover, was not Thoreau quite definite about what he
rejected: godless commercialism, blind patriotism,

ecological rapacity, et al.? Just as Socrates in
certain Platonic dialogues "merely" asks questions, acts
in a coy way, and leads the reader into some false
bottoms, but nonetheless with perfect clarity attacks
positions that he especially dislikes, so Thoreau
betrays his foundationalism in what he refutes as much
as in what he defends. My allegation in this book is
that Thoreau's memories of Socrates and Plato and the
neoplatonists are always just beneath the surface, and
are often on the surface, of his writing. He asks in
reference to the Greeks:

> Is my life vulgar, my fate mean,
>
> Which on these golden memories can
>
> lean?[78]

I think not.

Those who are familiar only with Plato's
denigration of art in the Republic may be surprised to
learn of the treatment of art as divine inspiration in
the Ion, and at my claim that Platonic metaphysics
provides a most helpful way to understand the most
profound uses of language in Thoreau. Mimesis can refer
not only to simple, imitative, representational uses of
language, but also to more abstract, symbolic uses that
aim at bridging the separation (chorismos) between

experienced reality and the higher (Platonic) region of
Forms and the Demiurge.[79] The very notion of a
linguistic symbol betrays <u>some</u> sort of ontological
duality between the familiar world and that less
familiar world that is symbolized, even though it is not
there (<u>me</u> <u>on</u>) to be directly experienced in the familiar
world. Thoreau's genius at least partially consists in
taking the higher world seriously without falling into
surrealism, whereby the world of experienced reality is
abandoned altogether. The "meontic" variety of <u>mimesis</u>
honors this world, even in its minutiae, while
transcending it through a participation (<u>methexis</u>),
albeit vicariously through words, in the higher realm of
Forms. Like the unfolding of a carpenter's rule, a
cantilevering of meaning, Thoreau's words receive their
meaning in the act of extension; the meaning of
Thoreau's words is marked on the rule itself to the
extent that we get closer to formal reality through
them. Simple <u>mimesis</u> can <u>arrest</u> the loss of being in
this cave of a world, but only meontic <u>mimesis</u> can
<u>restore</u> the wholeness of existence. Meontic activity is
instrumental in that there is no need for art in the
paradise of the <u>Republic</u>. Yet meontic activity is also

a consummatory "shimmering" in its own right, which
alleviates the diasparactive (diasparactos=torn to
pieces) burden of Thoreauvian fragmentation.

NOTES: CHAPTER FIVE

[1] Ralph Waldo Emerson, "Plato," in Representative Men (Boston: Houghton Mifflin, 1876), p. 42. It should be clear that I am using Emerson to better understand Thoreau. I am not trying to place Thoreau among the other transcendentalists for whom Platonic thought was important. This would be a much larger task than the one I have taken on in this book.

[2] Ibid., p. 41.

[3] Ibid., p. 43.

[4] Ibid., p. 54.

[5] Ibid., p. 56.

[6] Ibid., p. 75. As Epstein, p. 26, puts it, for Thoreau the animal in us is not to be extirpated, but "it" should be turned into an "I." Thoreau's poetizing of the wild, however, ensured that he would be the Moses of American vegetarianism, never entering into the promised land of a more consistent vegetarian practice.

[7] Emerson, "Plato," p. 85.

[8] Ibid., pp. 55, 71.

[9] Ibid., p. 44.

[10] Ibid., p. 74.

[11] Walden, p. 6.

[12] Ibid., pp. 321-322.

[13] Ibid., pp. 14-15, 56.

[14]Ibid., p. 56.

[15]Ibid., pp. 71, 123.

[16]Ibid., p. 140.

[17]Ibid., p. 8.

[18]Ibid., p. 79.

[19]Ibid., p. 90.

[20]Ibid., pp. 93-94. Millichap, p. 275, alerts us
to the fact that this mammoth cave is an allusion to
Mammoth Cave in Kentucky with its supposedly eyeless
fish; Thoreau has its dwellers with but a rudiment of an
eye, in Platonic fashion.

[21]Walden, pp. 95-96.

[22]Ibid., pp. 97-98.

[23]Ibid., p. 98.

[24]Ibid., p. 99.

[25]Ibid., p. 175.

[26]Ibid., pp. 188-189, 194.

[27]Ibid., pp. 214-215.

[28]Ibid., p. 222.

[29]Nikos Kazantzakis, Zorba the Greek, translated by
Carl Wildman (New York: Simon and Schuster, 1962), p.
66

[30]See my "Eating and Spiritual Exercises: Food for
Thought from Saint Ignatius and Nikos Kazantzakis,"

Christianity and Literature XXXIV (1983), pp. 25-32. On
the general relationship between nature and God see my
Not Even a Sparrow Falls: Hartshorne, God, and Animals,
forthcoming.

[31] Walden, p. 311.

[32] Ibid., p. 332.

[33] Ibid., p. 329.

[34] See Chapter Two, note 88.

[35] Walden, p. 324.

[36] Reform Papers, p. 88.

[37] Ibid., pp. 86-87.

[38] Writings, 11, pp. 4-5.

[39] Ibid., 7, p. 276. See Larry Bowden,
"Transcendence in Walden," Religion in Life 46 (1977),
pp. 166-171, who alerts us to the fact that for Thoreau
it is only by being vigorously awake that we can
penetrate beyond the surface of things, and discover not
only that nature is where we encounter the transcendent,
but that nature has an objective reality.

[40] Charles Hartshorne, "Mysticism and Rationalistic
Metaphysics," Monist 59 (1976), pp. 463-469.

[41] Susan Sontag, "Reflections on 'The Deputy'," in
Against Interpretation (New York: Farrar, Straus, and
Giroux, 1961), pp. 127-128. Contrast Sontag's idea with

the rather extreme view of William Gass: "Truth ...has
antipathy to art. It is best when a writer has a deep
and abiding indifference to it, although as a private
person it may be vital to him." Ironically, Gass is
like Plato in not trusting some artists. See Fiction &
the Figures of Life (Boston: Nonpareil, 1978), p. 8.

[42]Quoted in Sontag, "Against Interpretation,"
ibid., p. 5.

[43]Ibid., p. 6.

[44]Whether or not recent Freudian interpretations of
Thoreau would irk Sontag I do not know. See Raymond
Gozzi, ed., Thoreau's Psychology (Lanham, Maryland:
University Press of America, 1983); Richard Lebeaux,
Young Man Thoreau (Amherst: University of Massachusetts
Press, 1977) and Richard Lebeaux, Thoreau's Seasons
(Amherst: University of Massachusetts Press, 1984).
(Although I am not convinced by the studies in the Gozzi
volume that argue that Thoreau was a homosexual, if
indeed he were a homosexual he could not have failed to
notice the treatment of homosexual themes in Plato's
Symposium, for example, but also in the Charmides, etc.)

[45]Sontag, "Against Interpretation," p. 7.

[46]Those who think that Plato's own theory of art
was reactionary should read the excellent piece of

scholarship by Eric Havelock, Preface to Plato
(Cambridge:   Harvard University Press, 1963).

[47]Sontag, "Against Interpretation," p. 8.

[48]See my "The Virtue of Boldness," Spirituality
Today 37 (1985), 213-220.

[49]Cavell, p. 3.

[50]Ibid., p. 4.

[51]Ibid., p. 47.

[52]Ibid., p. 93, et al.

[53]Walden, p. 100.

[54]Ibid., pp. 325-326.

[55]Ibid., pp. 297, 299.

[56]Cavell, p. 94.

[57]Ibid., p. 54.

[58]Ibid., p. 110.

[59]Ibid., p. 112.

[60]Ibid., p. 55.

[61]Ibid., p. 109.  For example, it takes two to
engage in dialectical conversation or to have a
dialogue.  Plato suggests that this conversation can be
internal to each one of us.  See Sophist 263E, 264A, and
Theaeteus 189E.

[62]Ibid., p. 11.  Also see Mary Elkins Moller,
Thoreau in the Human Community (Amherst:   University of

Massachusetts Press, 1980).

[63]Cavell, p. 75.

[64]Cf. Cavell, p. 147.

[65]Ibid., p. 148.

[66]Ibid., p. 141.

[67]Ibid., p. 87; also see p. 115.

[68]Millichap, p. 279.

[69]See Jonathan Wordsworth, William Wordsworth: The Borders of Vision (Oxford: Oxford University Press, 1982), pp. 55, 66, 211, 213.

[70]See Kohák, pp. 52, 68.

[71]Journal, volume 2, pp. 162-165.

[72]Ibid., pp. 372-373.

[73]Ibid., pp. 366, 374.

[74]Ibid., pp. 168, 261, 320.

[75]Walter Benn Michaels, "Walden's False Bottoms," Glyph (Baltimore: Johns Hopkins, 1977).

[76]Walden, pp. 97-98.

[77]Ibid., p. 330.

[78]A Week, p. 55.

[79]In this last paragraph I have greatly benefited from the work of Thomas McFarland, Romanticism and the Forms of Ruin (Princeton: Princeton University Press, 1981), pp. 382-418.

# BIBLIOGRAPHY

I. Primary Sources.

    A. Plato.

        1. _Platonis Opera._ 5 volumes. Edited by
J. Burnet. Oxford: Clarendon Press,
1899-1907.

        2. _The Collected Dialogues of Plato._
Edited by Edith Hamilton and Huntington
Cairns. Princeton: Princeton
University Press, 1973.

        3. Taylor, Thomas. _Plato's Dialogues_
(1804). And _Miscellanies_ (1820).

    B. Thoreau.

        1. _The Writings of Henry D. Thoreau._
Princeton: Princeton University Press,
1971-. Referred to in the text by the
title to each volume: _Walden, A Week
on the Concord and Merrimack Rivers,
The Maine Woods, Reform Papers, Early
Essays and Miscellanies, Journal 1,_ and
_Journal 2._

2. The Writings of Henry David Thoreau.
   New York: AMS Press, 1968. Reprinted
   from the 1906 edition. Referred to in
   the text as Writings.

3. Harding, Walter, and Bode, Carl,
   editors. The Correspondence of Henry
   David Thoreau. New York: New York
   University Press, 1958.

4. Excursions. Boston: Houghton Mifflin,
   1883.

5. Bode, Carl, editor. Collected Poems of
   Henry David Thoreau. Baltimore: Johns
   Hopkins University Press, 1965.

II. Secondary Sources.

   Adams, Raymond. "Thoreau and Immortality."
          Studies in Philology 26 (1929).

   Attick, Richard. The Art of Literary Research.
          New York: Norton, 1963.

   Anderson, Charles R. The Magic Circle of Walden.
          New York: Holt, Rinehart, and Winston,
          1968.

   Bouffartigue and Patillon. Porphyre de l'
          abstinence. 3 volumes. Paris: 1977.

Bowden, Larry. "Transcendence in Walden."
Religion in Life 46 (1977).

Brehier, Emile. The Philosophy of Plotinus.
Chicago: University of Chicago Press,
1958.

Cameron, Kenneth Walter. Young Thoreau and the
Classics. Hartford: Transcendental
Books, 1975.

....Transcendental Apprenticeship: Notes on Young
Henry Thoreau's Reading. Hartford:
Transcendental Books, 1976.

Cavell, Stanley. The Senses of Walden. San
Francisco: North Point, 1981.
Originally published in 1972 by Viking.

Cook, Reginald. "Ancient Rites at Walden." In
Richard Ruland, editor, Twentieth
Century Interpretations of Walden.
Englewood Cliffs, New Jersey:
Prentice-Hall, 1968.

Cudworth, Ralph. The True Intellectual System of
the Universe. London: 1820. 4
volumes.

Dacier, Andre. The Life of Pythagoras. London:
1707.

Dombrowski, Daniel A.  "Rawls and Thoreau on Civil
Disobedience."  Thoreau Journal
Quarterly XI (1979).

....Plato's Philosophy of History.  Washington,
D.C.:  University Press of America,
1981.

...."Atlantis and Plato's Philosophy."  Apeiron XV
(1981).

...."Eating and Spiritual Exercises:  Food for
Thought from Saint Ignatius and Nikos
Kazantzakis."  Christianity and
Literature XXXIV (1983).

...."Vegetarianism and the Argument from Marginal
Cases in Porphyry."  Journal of the
History of Ideas XLV (March, 1984).

...."Lumen est umbra Dei, Deus est Lumen Luminis."
The Classical Bulletin 60 (Spring,
1984).

...."Was Plato a Vegetarian?"  Apeiron XVIII
(June, 1984).

....The Philosophy of Vegetarianism. Amherst:
        University of Massachusetts Press,
        1984; also Vegetarianism: The
        Philosophy Behind the Ethical Diet.
        London:  Thorsons, 1985.

...."Thoreau, Sainthood, and Vegetarianism."
        Forthcoming in The American
        Transcendental Quarterly.

Emerson, Ralph Waldo. "Plato." In Representative
        Men. Boston:  Houghton Mifflin, 1876.

...."Thoreau." In Reginald L. Cook, editor,
        Selected Prose and Poetry. New York:
        Holt, Rinehart, and Winston, 1969.

Epstein, Robert. "A Benefactor of His Race:
        Thoreau's 'Higher Laws' and the Heroics
        of Vegetarianism." Between the Species
        1 (Summer, 1985).

Eslick, Leonard. "The Dyadic Character of Being."
        Modern Schoolman 21 (1953-1954).

...."Plato as Dipolar Theist." Process Studies 12
        (1982).

Fergenson, Laraine. "Thoreau, Daniel Berrigan, and
        the Problem of Transcendental
        Politics." Soundings (Spring, 1982).

208

Foerster, Norman. "The Intellectual Heritage of
    Thoreau." In Richard Ruland, editor,
    Twentieth Century Interpretations of
    Walden. Englewood Cliffs, New Jersey:
    Prentice-Hall, 1968.

Garber, Frederick. Thoreau's Redemptive
    Imagination. New York: New York
    University Press, 1977.

Gass, William. Fiction & the Figures of Life.
    Boston: Nonpareil, 1978.

Gérando, Joseph Marie de. Histoire Comparée des
    Systèmes de Philosophie. 2nd edition.
    Paris: 1822-1823.

Gohdes, Clarence. "Henry Thoreau, Bachelor of
    Arts." Classical Journal XXIII
    (February, 1928).

Gozzi, Raymond, editor. Thoreau's Psychology.
    Lanham, Maryland: University Press of
    America, 1983.

Greeley, Horace. New York Tribune. June 13,
    1849. Also see Walter Harding, editor,
    Thoreau: A Century of Criticism.
    Dallas: Southern Methodist University
    Press, 1965.

Harding, Walter. _Thoreau's Library_.
Charlottesville: University of
Virginia Press, 1957.

...._The Variorum Walden_. New York: Twayne, 1962.

...._Emerson's Library_. Charlottesville:
University of Virginia Press, 1967.

...._The New Thoreau Handbook_. New York: New York
University Press, 1980.

Hartshorne, Charles. _Philosophers Speak of God_.
Chicago: University of Chicago Press,
1953.

...._Creative Synthesis and Philosophic Method_. La
Salle, Illinois: Open Court, 1970; and
London: SCM Press, 1970.

Haussleiter, Johannes. _Der Vegetarismus in der
antike_. Berlin: Topelmann, 1935.

Havelock, Eric. _Preface to Plato_. Cambridge:
Harvard University Press, 1963.

Howarth, William. _The Book of Concord: Thoreau's
Life as a Writer_. New York: Viking
Press, 1982.

Iamblichus. _Life of Pythagoras_. Translated by
Thomas Taylor. London: Valpy, 1818.

Jacobs, Frederick. The Greek Reader. Boston:
Hilliard, Gray, Little, and Wilkins,
1827.

Johnson, J. Prescott. "The Ontological Argument
in Plato." Personalist (Winter, 1963).

Jones, Joseph. "Transcendental Grocery Bills:
Thoreau's Walden and Some Aspects of
American Vegetarianism." University of
Texas Studies in English 36 (1957).

Kohák, Erazim. The Embers and the Stars: A
Philosophical Inquiry into the Moral
Sense of Nature. Chicago: University
of Chicago Press, 1984.

Krutch, Joseph. Henry David Thoreau. New York:
Dell, 1965.

Lebeaux, Richard. Young Man Thoreau. Amherst:
University of Massachusetts Press,
1977.

....Thoreau's Seasons. Amherst: University of
Massachusetts Press, 1984.

McFarland, Thomas. Romanticism and the Forms of
Ruin. Princeton: Princeton University
Press, 1981.

....Originality & Imagination. Baltimore: Johns
       Hopkins University Press, 1985.

Michaels, Walter Benn. "Walden's False Bottoms."
       Glyph. Baltimore: Johns Hopkins
       University Press, 1977.

Millichap, Joseph. "Plato's Allegory of the Cave
       and the Vision of Walden." English
       Language Notes 7 (June, 1970).

Moller, Mary Elkins. Thoreau in the Human
       Community. Amherst: University of
       Massachusetts Press, 1980.

More, Paul Elmer. The Religion of Plato.
       Princeton: Princeton University Press,
       1921.

...."A Hermit's Notes on Thoreau." In Walter
       Harding, editor, Thoreau: A Century of
       Criticism. Dallas: Southern Methodist
       University Press, 1965.

Newsome, David. Two Classes of Men: Platonism
       and English Romantic Thought. London:
       Murray, 1974.

Oehlschlaeger, Fritz, and Hendrick, George,
        editors, Toward the Making of Thoreau's
        Modern Reputation. Urbana: University
        of Illinois Press, 1979.

Paul, Sherman. The Shores of America. Urbana:
        University of Illinois Press, 1958.

Pickard, John B. "The Religion of 'Higher Laws'."
        In Richard Ruland, editor, Twentieth
        Century Interpretations of Walden.
        Englewood Cliffs, New Jersey:
        Prentice-Hall, 1968.

Plutarch's Morals. The translation by "several
        hands." 5th edition. London: 1718. 5
        volumes.

Porphyry. On Abstinence from Animal Food.
        Translated by Thomas Taylor. London:
        Centaur Press, 1965.

Rader, Melvin. Wordsworth: A Philosophical
        Approach. Oxford: Clarendon Press,
        1967.

Raine, Kathleen, and Harper, George Mills,
        editors, Thomas Taylor the Platonist.
        Princeton: Princeton University Press,
        1969.

Rawls, John. A Theory of Justice. Cambridge:
        Harvard University Press, 1971.

Regan, Tom. "Fox's Critique of Animal
        Liberation." Ethics 88 (January,
        1978).

Ritter, Heinrich. The History of Ancient
        Philosophy. Translated by A.J.W.
        Morrison. Oxford: 1838-1846.

Salomon, Louis B. "The Least-Remembered Alcott."
        New England Quarterly 34 (1961).

Salt, Henry S. The Life of Henry David Thoreau.
        1890.

Sanborn, F.B. The Life of Henry David Thoreau.
        1917.

Selectae e Veteri Testamento Historiae. Nova
        Editio. Londoni: Veneunt A. Millar, W.
        Law, et R. Cater, 1797.

Seybold, Ethel. The Quest and the Classics. New
        Haven: Yale University Press, 1951.

Shepard, Odell, editor. The Journals of Bronson
        Alcott. Boston: Little, Brown, 1938.

Singer, Peter. Animal Liberation. New York: New
        York Review, 1975.

Sontag, Susan. Against Interpretation. New York:
        Farrar, Straus, and Giroux, 1961.

Thorpe, Willard. "The Huckleberry Party."
        Thoreau Society Bulletin (Summer,
        1952).

Tufts, Marshall. A Tour Through College. 1832.
        And The Ancient and Popular
        Pneumatology.

Urmson, J.O. "Saints and Heroes." In A.I.
        Melden, editor, Essays in Moral
        Philosophy. Seattle: University of
        Washington Press, 1958.

Wagenknecht, Edward. Henry David Thoreau: What
        Manner of Man? Amherst: University of
        Massachusetts Press, 1981.

Whitehead, A.N. "Peace." In Adventures of Ideas.
        New York: Macmillan, 1933.

Wolf, William J. Thoreau: Mystic, Prophet,
        Ecologist. Philadelphia: Pilgrim
        Press, 1974.

Wordsworth, Jonathan. William Wordsworth: The
        Borders of Vision. Oxford: Oxford
        University Press, 1982.

## INDEX OF NAMES

Adam 67

Adams, R. 7, 18, 39,
   68-69, 140

Alcibiades 70

Alcott, B. 96, 101, 110,
   112, 156

Alcott, W.A. 121, 158-159

Alexander the Great 158

Altherr, T. 164

Altick, R. 21

Anderson, C. 10, 20, 35,
   67, 75-78, 103, 109,
   111, 119, 121-122,
   155, 157-159, 164

Anselm, St. 79, 89, 105

Apollo 122, 159

Aratus 166

Archimedes 101

Aristophanes 50

Aristotle 53, 82, 89,
   100, 118, 146

Atropos 72

Augustine, St. 82

Bentham, J. 124, 160

Berrigan, D. 65

Bowden, L. 199

Brehier, E. 158

Cameron, K. 5, 8, 17-19,
   21, 72, 103, 158

Carlyle, T. 53, 57

Cavell, S. 66, 108, 184-
   186, 201-202

Channing, W.E. 7, 11, 18,
   59, 105

Child, L.M. 8

Cicero 17

Clinias 152

Clotho 72

Coleridge, S.T. 1, 110

Confucius 158

Cook, R. 18

Cronus, 147-149

Cudworth, R. 9, 19

Dacier, A. 9, 19

Demiurge 100, 109, 138

Derrida, J. 181

Dicaerchus 166

Diodorus Siculus 166

Diogenes 69

Diogenes Laertius 163

Eleatic Stranger 97

Emerson, R.W. 1, 15, 20,
72, 77, 104, 110, 118-
119, 157, 159, 167-
170, 189, 192, 197

Empedocles 32, 166

Ephorus 166

Epstein, R. 164, 197

Eros 99

Eslick, L. 98-99,
108

Eve 67

Farmer, J. 175-176

Fergenson, L. 65

Foerster, N. 11-13, 20,
156

Fogle, R.H. 110

Francis of Assissi, St.
133

Franklin, B. 10, 121

Frye, N. 21

Gandhi, 45-46

Garber, F. 155

Gass, W. 200

Gerando, J.M. de 8, 19

Glaucon 40

Gohdes, C. 18

Gozzi, R. 200

Greeley, H. 77-78, 103

Harding, W. 18, 20, 64,
68-69, 103-104, 106-
107, 163

Harper, G.M. 65

Hartshorne, C. 64, 75,
78-82, 84-86, 88-91,
94, 97-99, 101, 104-
105, 107, 109, 137,
139, 179, 199

Haussleiter, J. 146-147,
166

Havelock, E. 201

Hesiod 166

Hochhuth, R. 180

Homer 5, 12

Hosmer, E. 38

Howarth, W. 49, 70

Iamblichus 6, 8-9, 56, 59, 121-122, 146, 159

Icarus 31

Ignatius, St. 198

Jacobs, F. 17

Jesus 76

Johnson, J.P. 64, 105

Jones, J. 111, 119, 121, 155-159

Jones, S.A. 71

Kazantzakis, N. 175, 198

King, M.L. 45-46

Kohák, E. 139, 162, 202

Kolbe, Fr. 115

Krutch, J. 77-78, 103

Lachesis 72

Lebeaux, R. 200

McFarland, T. 21, 202

Mencius 132

Menu 158

Michaels, W.B. 189-191, 202

Mill, J.S. 115-116

Millichap, J. 18, 20, 60, 65, 74, 198, 202

Moller, M.E. 201

More, P.E. 77, 104, 108

Moses 197

Murray, H. 158

Newsome, D. 3

Nietzsche, F. 181

Ovid 166

Paley, W. 48

Parmenides 98

Paul, S. 71

Paul, St. 158

Pickard, J. 76, 78, 101, 103, 110, 117, 157

Plotinus 8-9, 27, 64, 100, 146, 158, 166

Plutarch 8, 19

Polis, J. 91

Porphyry 6, 8-9, 20, 35, 67, 121-123, 125, 146, 159-160, 166

Pythagoras 8-9, 19, 31-32, 56, 59, 122, 146, 152,

155-156, 158-159, 163, 171

Rader, M. 3

Raine, K. 65

Raleigh, W. 9, 26, 63-65, 77

Rawls, J. 44-45, 47-49, 69-70

Regan, T. 125, 160

Ritter, H. 8, 19

Rorty, R. 108

Salomon, L. 159

Salt, H. 50, 70-71, 111-112, 156, 159

Sanborn, F.B. 73

Seybold, E. 5-7, 9-10, 17-20, 67, 69-70, 111, 122, 155, 157, 159

Shanley, J. 20

Sidney, P. 21

Singer, P. 124, 133, 145, 156, 160, 162-163, 165

Socinus 109-110

Socrates 5, 8, 10, 17, 24,
33, 35, 42-43, 46-49, 55, 57, 69, 73, 150-151, 159, 169-170, 184, 186, 193

Sontag, S. 180-184, 199-201

Spinoza 89

Taylor, T. 1, 6, 29, 35, 64-66, 108, 159

Teilhard de Chardin 107

Thales 166

Theophrastus 166

Thomas Aquinas, St. 82-83

Thoreau, J. 38

Thoreau, S. 96

Thorpe, W. 77-78, 103

Tufts, M. 9, 19

Urmson, J.O. 113-114, 116, 130, 143, 156-157

Wagenknecht, E. 155

Whitehead, A.N. 60, 74, 107

Wolf, W. 20, 39, 50, 69,

71, 94-95, 101, 103-
104, 106-108, 110,
136, 157, 158, 162

Wordsworth, J. 202

Wordsworth, W. 1, 34, 68,
100, 103, 109-110, 180,
189

World-Soul 100, 108-109, 138

Paul Schuchmann

# ARISTOTLE AND THE PROBLEM OF MORAL DISCERNMENT

European University Studies: Series XX, Philosophy. Vol. 62
ISBN 3-261-04681-3                164 pp.                br. US $ 17,70

recommended prices - alterations reserved

The present study represents a preliminary philosophical interpretation of the concept of moral discernment or phronesis in the 'Ethics' of Aristotle. Taking his standpoint from certain trends in contemporary transcendental philosophy, the author suggests s possible approach to the problem of the norm for moral and political judgment in Aristotle's thought. Relevant texts from the 'Ethics' are interpreted within an ontological context, and a brief criticism of traditional viewpoints is presented.

Contents: Introduction. — Interpretation: Agathon, Eudaimonia, Ethos, Dianoia, Kalon — Critique. Appendix I: Aristotle's Phronesis Transcendental Thinking: The View of Bernard Lonergan. — Appendix II: Aristotle's Phronesis and Contemporary Hermeneutics: The View of Hans–Georg Gadamer.— Selected Bibliography.

PETER LANG PUBLISHING, INC.
62 West 45th Street
USA - New York, NY 10036